MUNCIE

&

DELAWARE COUNTY

MUNCIE

&

DELAWARE COUNTY

AN ILLUSTRATED RETROSPECTIVE

WILEY W. SPURGEON, JR.

"PARTNERS IN PROGRESS" BY H. DUANE HARRISON

PRODUCED IN COOPERATION WITH THE
MUNCIE-DELAWARE COUNTY CHAMBER OF COMMERCE

WINDSOR PUBLICATIONS, INC.
WOODLAND HILLS, CALIFORNIA

Endpapers: An 1872 Bird's Eye View of Muncie, Indiana, *looks southeast from White River at High Street. Courtesy, Indiana State Library*

Page two: Crowds of people jammed Walnut Street (seen looking north toward Jackson), apparently for a parade or rally in the days before automobiles were in evidence. All of the buildings, many greatly altered, are still standing today; most were constructed between 1880 and 1900. Courtesy, E.F. Petty

Page six: Industrial development in the south part of Muncie led to a need for increased fire protection in the 1890s. At first a single station at Jefferson and Willard streets handled fires in the entire territory. A few years later similar stations were built at Willard and Ebright and at Willard and Council (shown). Each had a hose cart and a paid crew on duty. These stations—with motorized equipment—survived until the 1960s. From the author's collection

Windsor Publications, Inc.
History Book Division

Publisher: John M. Phillips
Staff for *Muncie and Delaware County: An Illustrated Retrospective:*
Editor and Picture Editor: Laurel H. Paley
Editorial Director, Corporate Biographies: Karen Story
Design Director: Alexander D'Anca
Assistant Director, Corporate Biographies: Phyllis Gray
Editor, Corporate Biographies: Judith Hunter
Editorial Assistants: Lonnie Pham, Patricia Buzard, Pat Pittman, Susan Wells
Composing: E. Beryl Myers, Barbara Neiman
Proofreading: Doris R. Malkin
Production Art: Beth Bowman
Marketing Director: Ellen Kettenbeil
Sales Manager: Bob Moffitt
Sales Coordinator: Joan Baker
Sales Representative: Jim Koch

Library of Congress Cataloging in Publication Data

Spurgeon, Wiley W.
  Muncie & Delaware County

  Partners in progress / by H. Duane Harrison: p.
  Bibliography: p.
  Includes index.
  1. Muncie (Ind.)—History.   2. Muncie (Ind.)—
Description.   3. Delaware County (Ind.)—History.
4. Delaware County (Ind.)—Description and travel.
5. Muncie (Ind.)—Industries.   6. Delaware County
(Ind.)—Industries.   I. Harrison, H. Duane.
II. Muncie-Delaware County Chamber of Commerce.
III. Title: Muncie and Delaware County.

F534.M9S68   1984   977.2'65   84-15249
ISBN 0-89781-104-6

THIS VOLUME IS DEDICATED TO
RICHARD A. AND MILDRED C. GREENE,
WHO IN THEIR LIFETIMES HAVE DONE MORE
THAN ANY OTHER PEOPLE
OR GROUPS OF PEOPLE TO MAKE US AWARE OF,
AND APPRECIATE,
OUR LOCAL HISTORICAL HERITAGE.

Contents

Acknowledgments

Some years ago the Dynamo Club, an organization within the Muncie Commercial Club, adopted for the city the slogan 'Muncie, the Magic City.' Less positive slogans suggested in intervening years have not endured as well because there is a special magic in Muncie and the surrounding area, evidenced by residents' strong sense of personal roots, patriotism, deep religious convictions, and belief in honest work as the route to success. This book is a tribute to that magic.

A growing awareness of, and interest in, our area's history are the factors that have made this publication possible. There has been no history of Delaware County published in book form since the early 1920s. This publication does not pretend to be a scholarly history, but rather an overview in pictures and text of the Muncie and Delaware County community over a period of nearly 200 years.

Special thanks must be conveyed to Charles Stroh, former president of the Muncie-Delaware County Chamber of Commerce, and Kelly Stanley, Waldo F. Beebe, Merlin Knauss, and Richard Nelson of the chamber. The chamber should be congratulated for its willingness to take on a pictorial history as a corporate project, endorse it, and nurture its development. James E. Watkins, Jr., who suggested to the writer that he might be an appropriate person to prepare the history, also must be thanked.

Whitney, Thomas, Daniel, and Sunny Spurgeon have also been most understanding and supportive, and the latter must also be recognized for her assistance in obtaining information about and pictures of local hospital and medical history.

Cinda Inman did the original manuscript from a typewritten draft that was heavily edited. When it came out or her word processor, it was in beautiful shape for sending along to the publisher.

Laurel Paley of Windsor Publications has been an extremely helpful and patient editor. Ruth Chin has kept smiling despite demands for her services as a photographer on an almost instantaneous basis more than once. And at People's Studio all personnel were most helpful in copying and reprinting numerous historic photographs. Assistance and advice in reproducing historic documents were provided by J.E. Murcia, William Proctor, James Wyatt, Dave Peckinpaugh, Richard Coalter, and David Douthitt, all of *The Muncie Star* and *Muncie Evening Press*.

Certainly there could be no pictorial history if people did not preserve photographs and make them available. Special thanks go to all of these individuals and organizations, as indicated by the credits by individual photographs in the book. Edmund F. Petty, Jeffrey Koenker, Richard and Mildred Greene, Ernest Parkison, and Douglas Bakken (of Ball Brothers Foundation) were especially helpful in the pursuit of photographs.

The Stoeckel Delaware County Archives of Ball State University are unusually well suited to the type of research and picture research that I did for this book. Nancy Turner there was especially helpful, as was David Tambo, director. The late Althea Stoeckel herself, a remarkable lady and historian, brought to Muncie in the 1960s the realization that we had a historical heritage that might slip away if we did not work to preserve it. Numerous of her Ball State University colleagues have carried the torch for this mission, especially Dwight Hoover, now director of the Center for Middletown Studies, Thomas Sargent, associate dean of the College of Sciences and Humanities, Ross Johnson, David Tambo's predecessor, and Marie Fraser, director of Public Information Services. I would also like to thank Marie Fraser for reading this manuscript critically after its final editing.

Certainly, special acknowledgment goes to Becky Lamirand, who has handled the author's business secretarial duties so effectively for the past four years, for all the time and effort that she has contributed to this and other labors of love and duty. A similar acknowledgment goes, finally, to Eugene S. Pulliam, publisher of *The Muncie Star* and *Muncie Evening Press*, for indulging a project like this and letting his Muncie executive editor pursue it.

Wiley W. Spurgeon, Jr.
Muncie
August 1984

CHAPTER I

Taming the Wilderness

The terrain of what would become Delaware County, although beautiful, proved to be a challenge to early Indian and white settlers. From Parker Gillmore, Prairie Farms and Prairie Folk *volume I, 1872*

The geography of Delaware County reflects to a great extent the effect of the glaciers that once covered a large part of the North American continent. Because of its location near the southern end of glacial activity, the county has many gravelly ridges, deposited as the ice melted and eventually retreated.

The northwest quarter of the county contains the only true prairie, also glacial-originated, since part of the scouring action of the ice can be credited for the deep topsoil and swamps that the first settlers found in the area in the early 1800s.

Early civilizations—called Mound Builders by later archeologists— probably lived along the west fork of the White River, evidenced by the burial mounds that they left behind. Later Indian tribes such as the Miami may have descended from these peoples, but little remains to tie them to Delaware County after the eighth century.

Thus, as late as 200 years ago, the area now known as Delaware County was a wilderness, untracked and virtually uninhabited.

There is no recorded account of any exploration of east central Indiana by French Jesuit missionaries, who came into the area south of the Great Lakes in the late 17th and early 18th centuries. Fur traders mingled with the missionaries there in the last half of the 17th century, although most trading was carried on in part of what is now Canada, east of Lake Huron and north of lakes Erie and Ontario.

One of these traders was René Robert Cavelier, Sieur de La Salle. Reaching Quebec, he heard tales about the land to the southwest and decided to explore it, perhaps finding a route to the Pacific. In several years of explorations La Salle did not find the nonexistent river to the southwest, but he did visit northern Indiana, and it was primitive exploration like his that placed the entire area—now the states of Ohio, Indiana, Illinois, Michigan, and Wisconsin—firmly under the French flag for nearly a century.

After the French and Indian War, control over the Northwest Territories passed from France to Britain with the 1763 Treaty of Paris. Then, during the Revolutionary War, the region became the property of the new United States of America.

In 1775 Virginian General George Rogers Clark had begun a campaign to win British military posts in the Northwest Territories. Clark took Kaskaskia, Illinois, without a struggle, and peacefully convinced French residents of Vincennes that their lot would be better with the colonists than with the British. Later battles confirmed the campaign's success, and the second Treaty of Paris was signed in 1783, ending the Revolution and recognizing the former colonies and their territories—including Clark's "conquests"—as an independent nation.

Later, under the Northwest Ordinances of 1783 and 1787 passed by the new Congress under the Articles of Confederation, the machinery was set in place for settlement of what would eventually become five new states. The land was to be surveyed and made available for settlement. Slavery was barred. A governmental system was established, the Indians' right to their land was to be respected (subject to negotiation or payment), education was to be encouraged, and the basic freedoms enjoyed by United States citizens were conferred on territorial residents.

It was as the new nation was being formed that Indians began again to settle in what is now Delaware County. The county received its name from these Indians, the Leni Lenape or Delaware, who had lived along the river of that name in the states of Delaware, Pennsylvania, and New Jersey. As colonists settled the western portion of these areas in the 18th century, the Indians were pushed first into western Pennsylvania and later, as that area too was claimed by settlers, into what is now Ohio. Settlers followed into Ohio, their journey made easier west of Pittsburgh by the navigable Ohio River, so the Delawares moved into what is now eastern Indiana and established several villages along White River, which they called Wapahani. They stayed out of the way of the dominant Miamis, who lived further north.

Two significant Delaware villages existed in what is now Delaware County. One of these villages, of the Munsee or "Wolf" clan of the Delaware, was located at the northernmost bend of the river, at or near the current site of the Minnetrista Orchards, about a mile north of what is now the center of Muncie. Some three-and-a-half miles southeast, the other village was called Buckongahelastown, now marked as Old Town Hill on Burlington Drive.

Buckongahelastown was named for the influential Delaware chief Buckongahelas. He and Miami chief Little Turtle had fought with British assistance against generals St. Clair and Wayne, who had been trying to secure the United States' new Northwest Territory after the Revolution. Buckongahelas later shifted his position to advocate peaceful relations between the Indians and the United States. He died in 1804, a year before the Shawnee brothers Tecumseh and The Prophet organized a hostile Indian confederation in Indiana. Although the four-year-old Indiana Territory had barely been settled, the brothers opposed any further white intrusions onto Indian lands.

The United States government had already begun to enter into treaties with Indian nations to make land available for entry by U.S. citizens. The first of these treaties, the 1795 Treaty of Greenville, opened southeast Indiana and much of southern Ohio. Indians who resided on these lands

Right: This map of the Northwest Territory, taken from Mathew Carey's American Pocket Atlas *of 1801, was the first map to use the name "Indiana" while referring to the area that would become the state. Courtesy, Indiana Historical Society*

Far right, top: A very rare pen-and-ink drawing from the mid-17th century shows the dress and weapons of an early Leni Lenape family. Delaware County was named for the Leni Lenape or Delaware Indians, who began to settle its land in the 18th century. From Hiram Shenk, Encyclopedia of Pennsylvania, *1932*

Far right, bottom: Before it was given its west and north boundaries by the Indiana Legislature in 1827, Delaware County was the unsettled area west of Randolph County and north of Henry County. Southern Indiana was settled from the Ohio River northward and from the Ohio state line westward. The state capital was moved from Corydon, Harrison County, to Indianapolis, Marion County, in 1818 in anticipation of the state's future growth. Courtesy, Hoosier Heritage Press

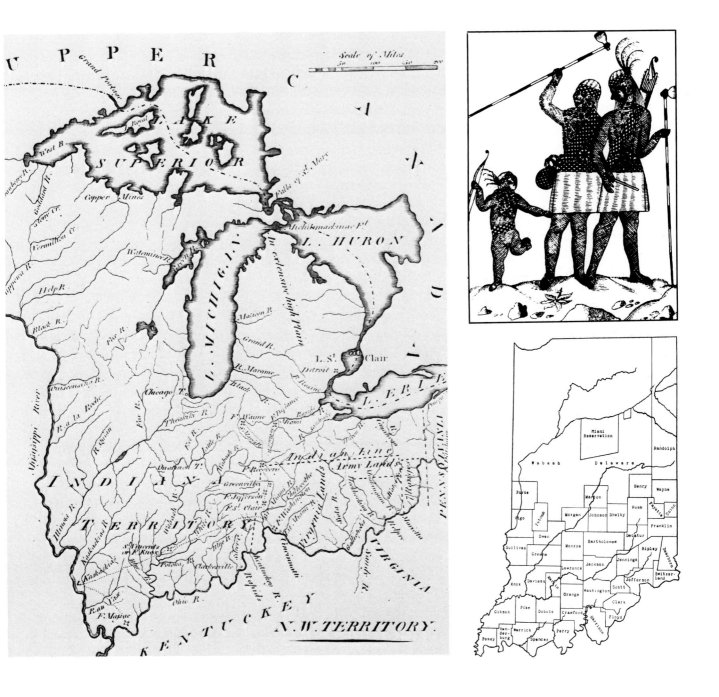

Above: Delaware County would have been in the state of Saratoga or perhaps Metropotamia and not Indiana if this late 18th century plan to divide the Northwest Territory had been followed by Congress. Map by E.V. Shockley. Courtesy, Hoosier Heritage Press

Opposite page: Kurtz & Allison of Chicago published this engraving of the Battle of Tippecanoe in 1889. Inaccurate and highly romanticized, the picture nevertheless demonstrates the popularity nationwide of the battle and its victorious General William Henry Harrison. Courtesy, Indiana State Library

moved to lands further west.

However, the Indian confederation proved a menace to settlers of the northwest (plus Indians' efforts to harass the settlers carried the tacit consent and aid of the British). Therefore William Henry Harrison, governor of the Indiana Territory, marched troops to Prophet's Town. General Harrison's forces defeated the militant Indians at the Battle of Tippecanoe.

It was not until the 1818 Treaty of St. Mary's that the area of Delaware County was secured for entry by white settlers. The treaty provided for the purchase from various tribes of most of the remaining Indian land south of the Wabash River. The Delawares agreed to move west of the Mississippi, while the Miamis agreed to remain north of the Wabash. The transaction was commonly called the New Purchase in Indiana. In addition, the New Purchase contained several "reservations" for a few individual Indians or their descendants, the most famous that of Rebecca Hackley, daughter of Williams Wells, the white son-in-law of Little Turtle. It contained 672 acres—a legal "section" of land plus 32 extra acres to compensate for unusable land under the waters of White River—and included the site of the Delawares' former Munsee village. It came to be known as the Hackley Reserve. By and large, however, the 1818 treaty provided for the expropriation of east and south central Indiana's Indians over a period of three years. The Delawares began their move to the west in the fall of 1820, passing Kaskaskia in southern Illinois in October.

The pioneers who came to Delaware County found that little had been done in advance by the Indians or the occasional white person living among them to tame the wilderness. The land was heavily forested, populated by bears and wolves along with other wild animals and birds. Rivers and streams provided the only highways, as paths had not yet been hacked through the woods.

However, the new settlers were not afraid of hard work. Because the Northwest Ordinance prohibited slavery, the pioneers tended to be farmers, people who did their own preparation and tilling of the land, as opposed to planters, large landowners who had hired help or slaves do the work.

John S. Ellis, in his 1898 book *Complete History of Delaware County, Indiana*, tells of early Perry Township settlers Cornelius Van Arsdoll, James Lee, William Blount, and David and Aaron Richardson,

who came with ox teams, cutting their road most of the way through the forest to their intended future homes, where they arrived in April . . . 1820. Arriving at this season of the year gave them the advantage of the spring and summer weather in which to clear off ground and erect their cabins. Their food at this early day consisted principally of bread and meat. The bread being often obtained by mashing corn between two stones. . . . the mashed grain was then sifted and prepared for baking. Game being abundant, the pioneer had no trouble in procuring meat. . . . squirrel, wild turkey, venison or opossum.

Land entries were usually made for a quarter-section, or 160 acres. Although, as the area filled, the proximity of a neighbor on the next quarter-section tended to diminish the isolated nature of pioneer life, neighbors could be depended on for help in major tasks like cutting and hauling timber, home- or barn-building, and harvesting.

Thus settlers who succeeded the Delaware Indians in the New Purchase tamed their tracts on both an individual and a collective basis. It was only after the land was tamed—by clearing, tilling, cutting, and farming—to a point beyond where mere survival was ensured that organized communities began in the wilderness that was to become Delaware County.

CHAPTER II

Pioneer Dreams and Victories

Hardships that winter brought to the already harsh pioneer life are in no way reflected in this highly idealized Currier & Ives lithograph, A Home in the Wilderness. *Why is the woodpile so skimpy, the baby bare-armed, and the cabin door open? However, few accurate illustrations of the period exist: early settlers were probably too busy surviving to try recording their surroundings and life-style.*

The first 35 years or so of Delaware County's existence were to be as an agricultural area, growing slowly in population, gradually raising more than it could itself consume, and counting each year less and less undeveloped wilderness.

Prior to 1822, when a land office was established at Fort Wayne to keep track of the entries being made into the area of the New Purchase, area settlers had to deal with land offices in Brookville, in southeastern Indiana, or in Jeffersonville, far to the south along the Ohio River. This may be the reason that records of settlement by individuals, like those of Perry Township's original pioneers, predate by many years the official land entries for the same tracts.

The first land entry in 1820 actually stemmed from another of the Treaty of St. Mary's reservations, that of Samuel Casman, a half-breed who had lived among the Indians in the area for some time. In the treaty Casman was granted a half-section of land, along with three other persons. Two other individuals were granted quarter sections. The grants were to be made official in the form of a land entry for them and their heirs after the land was surveyed. Casman's land, located where Buck Creek meets White River west of Muncie, was later sold to Oliver H. Smith. Land entries were subsequently made in all of the county's 12 townships in the 1820s and 1830s. Some sections in the county did not get their first official land entries until as late as 1837, so the populating of the region can be seen to have been a slow process.

One of the early settlers—and there is still debate as to where he actually first settled—was New Yorker Goldsmith C. Gilbert. He may have operated trading posts at several locations along Prairie Creek and/ or the Mississinewa River, dealing with the new settlers of the 1820s and Indians who had not yet moved west.

In the early 1820s Gilbert's trading post—presumed to be along the Mississinewa in Washington Township—was burned in an apparent act of Indian vandalism. Gilbert received $960 in damages, perhaps from the tribe but more likely from the federal government. He used this money to purchase the Hackley Reserve. According to legend (attributed to Indian inhabitants of the area and often repeated by later settlers), the land was desirable because its location in the bend of the river protected it from high winds or tornadoes. Similar legends exist for similarly located land in other parts of the nation. In any event, Gilbert acquired the land at slightly less than six dollars per acre and moved his trading operations

there probably in 1825 or 1826. He enjoyed good trade in the new location, and other settlers were attracted there.

Until Delaware County was established, the area was politically part of Randolph County, to the east. It was nine years after the treaty of St. Mary's, seven years after the first land entry, and 11 years after Indiana became a state, that Delaware County had a sufficient number of people to be organized as its own political entity on April 1, 1827, by legislative act.

By the time county government was established, there already were perhaps 600 people in what its inhabitants had decided to call Muncietown. A townsite was platted that year.

Other Indiana counties can refer in their history to lively fights over the location of the county seat, some involving gunfire and injury. Delaware County can claim no such fight. When the county was declared a separate entity, Goldsmith Gilbert and two other Muncietown residents, Lemuel Jackson and William Brown, donated 50 acres to the county to provide a seat for its government and institutions. Their offer was accepted; the records, which are sparse, show no other offers.

Because April 1, 1827, fell on a Sunday, Delaware County did not actually begin to function politically until the next day, when a citizens' assembly chose William Van Matre to be auditor, clerk, and recorder; John and Lewis Rees, associate judges; Peter Nolin, sheriff; and Valentine Gibson, Aaron Stout, and Enoch Nation, justices of the peace. The latter three also conducted the county's business until 1830, when the job of justice of the peace was separated from that of county commissioner by the legislature.

In 1828 the justices commissioned a courthouse, called by historian G.W.H. Kemper "a large and splendid building for that time." The two-story frame structure was used for perhaps 10 years following its completion in 1829. However, not all the land donated by Gilbert, Brown, and Jackson was used for county buildings and institutions; much was sold off by the county justices to individuals seeking sites for businesses and homes, and the funds were used to provide county officials means to run their offices.

Muncie and Delaware County entered the decade of the 1830s— probably the last decade which one could accurately call a true pioneer period—with county government organized, the countryside filling up with settlers, and the establishment of some of the amenities one might associate more with civilized life.

The National Road, projected nearly a quarter of a century previously to connect the states east of the Alleghenies with the new territory to the west, was completed to Wayne County in 1827. Primitive as it was, it opened the way for settlers to reach east central Indiana more easily. Eventually the National Road would be used to transport Indiana's surplus farm crops east, providing the newly settled areas with a favorable balance of trade.

Somewhat slower to arrive in Delaware County was free education. Despite the provisions of the Northwest Ordinances for the sale of certain territorial lands to provide funds for schools, the state of Indiana did not have a free school system until 1850. This came about only because of a perceived problem with citizen literacy in the 1830s and 1840s. In Delaware County in 1840, for example, in a population of 8,843, some 366 were illiterate. By the next census 10 years later, in a population of 10,976, the number of illiterates had climbed to 1,069!

Indeed, during the election of 1848, ballots included a public referendum about taxation for educational purposes. The vote in Delaware County was 808 to 715 against such taxation, and similar anti-school-tax votes were recorded in neighboring Henry, Madison, and Wayne counties (voters in Randolph, Grant, Jay, and Blackford counties favored the tax). Statewide, the vote favored the tax, and thus free tax-supported schools eventually came about.

Delaware County's first school was established in Perry Township in the same year that the county was formed. It was described as a rough building of hewn logs, heated by a fireplace, with windows covered with greased paper in the absence of glass, and a chimney made of mud and sticks. It was strictly a local effort, undertaken to educate the young of those who erected the building.

Muncietown had its first school beginning in the winter of 1829-1830 as did Salem Township, and Mount Pleasant Township joined the school move in 1831. Other townships added schools in the 1830s, although tax support would not come for more than a decade.

There undoubtedly were religious services in many homes in the years prior to 1829, and certainly some of these services must have involved traveling clergymen of one or another faith. In addition, the Methodists began conducting services in the courthouse in 1829. The first building to be used as a church was one constructed by the Methodists at Washington and Elm streets in 1839.

However, Delaware County had its first physician in advance of its first recorded church service or organized class in school. Dr. Dickinson Burt was on hand at least by August 1829 when he became Muncietown's second postmaster, operating both the post office and his medical practice from his house on Mulberry Street near Gilbert Street. In the 1830s the countryside was still something of a wilderness. Another early physician, Dr. Levi Minshall, writing about making house calls on horseback in the mid-1830s, described riding to his patients' homes in the middle of the river—with a clear view of each side—when the shallowness of the water permitted. That way, if marauding bears or wolves began pursuing him, he had a better chance to see them coming and get away.

The 1830s, a decade of continued land settlement, town-platting, road-building, and upgrading of social institutions, was also a decade of

Opposite page: Goldsmith C. Gilbert (top) was one of Muncie's most prominent early settlers. Purchaser of the Hackley Reserve and promoter of the town—first as the site of his trading post and soon afterward as the seat of government for the new Delaware County—Gilbert was chosen to represent the district in the Indiana Legislature. Born in the cabin that Gilbert had built near where Wysor and Walnut streets intersect today, Gilbert's daughter Mary Jane (bottom) was said to be the first female white child born in Muncie. From T.B. Helm, History of Delaware County, Indiana, *1881*

A contract for the county's second courthouse was awarded in 1837, and this stately building was erected in the square to replace the first courthouse across High Street to the west. The second building served until the 1880s, supplemented by an additional structure built in 1848. The square was beautified in the 1840s with fences and trees. Courtesy, Ball Stores, Inc.

commercial optimism.

The state of Indiana, following the example of its neighbors to the east, embarked on a large interal improvements program during the decade, mainly to improve transportation. Key to this program would be roads and canals, since the impact of railroads had not yet reached the states in "the west" and canals were thought to be more efficient and easier to build.

Optimism abounded. By 1837 Muncietown had a newspaper, *The Muncietonian*, published by David Gharkey, an early settler and entrepreneur. According to Muncie boosters, Muncietown was on its way to becoming a major commercial center. The Whitewater Canal, paralleling the Whitewater River northwest into Indiana from Lawrence-burg on the Ohio River, was eventually to be dug to Muncie. (Actually, it never progressed north of Hagerstown in Wayne County.) The state's Internal Improvement Act of 1836 proposed the Central Canal, with $3.5 million appropriated, to connect the Wabash and Erie near Fort Wayne with Indianapolis, preferably via Muncie. It also provided for a canal or railroad to connect the Central Canal and the Whitewater, also via Muncie. Nothing was built. (Although some digging was done in Salem Township, the effort was only token.)

To finance this improvement program, the state used funds gained from the sale of Indian lands and went irretrievably into debt besides. But as settlers continued to come and other counties continued to be opened for settlement, the area's agriculture became a business proposition, rather than one of survival.

Many Delaware County towns were platted in the 1830s. Some still exist. Some thrived briefly and died. Still others never made it past the platbook stage.

Yorktown, platted by Oliver H. Smith, actually existed before 1830, at which date a sawmill had been built at Buck Creek and White River. The first house in the community is believed to date to 1834.

As early as 1828 a mill had been built at Smithfield—platted in Liberty Township by David Stout and William Duncan—and a settlement developed there in the next few years. Smithfield's importance waned after the railroad passed it by. Then Selma, on the line built from Bellefontaine to Indianapolis through Muncie in 1852, became the township's commercial center.

Daleville owes its beginning in the 1830s to the proposed canal which Delaware Countians hoped would eventually connect the area to the Wabash and Erie Canal or to Indianapolis. There was a settlement north of the present townsite on the opposite side of White River along perhaps a mile of canal, but it foundered and disappeared, reverting to farm land.

Granville, a hamlet in Niles Township, dates to 1836 when a few residents clustered their houses along the Mississinewa River after the brief existence of Georgetown, which was founded perhaps a mile upriver

Residents of Perry Township built Delaware County's first schoolhouse (above left) in 1827, before the county itself was established. By 1879 Delaware County had 124 schoolhouses outside Muncie, including this one from Center Township (above). From T.B. Helm, History of Delaware County, Indiana, 1881

in 1833 and lasted only a few years.

Wheeling, still in existence in Washington Township along the Mississinewa, began as Cranberry Post Office, a site along the road through the wilderness between Muncie and Marion. A mile to the northeast Joseph Wilson founded Elizabethtown in the 1830s, naming it after his daughter. He hoped it would become the seat of a new county to include the area to the north combined with the three townships in northern Delaware County: Washington, Union, and Niles. But the legislature formed Blackford County north of Delaware County, leaving the Delaware County boundaries alone. Elizabethtown, left out of the county its boosters had hoped it would dominate, ultimately withered and disappeared.

Perry Township was the site of numerous early land entries because of its proximity to Wayne, Henry, and Randolph counties, and New Burlington developed as the township's retail center in the late 1830s. George Ribble platted the village, John Newcomb opened a general store, and Charles Newcomb started a tavern that became a popular spot along the road between Richmond and Muncie.

Albany, first located in Delaware Township, has in recent years grown northward into Niles Township and into Randolph County. Albany was platted in the 1830s and 1833 is the date given for its official beginning, on land purchased for the government by William Venard in 1832.

By the 1840s much of the wilderness had disappeared and the country-side was dotted with communities. The population had increased 10-fold from that when the county was established in 1827. There were roads, schools and churches. Although agriculture would continue to dominate the area for another quarter century, events were taking place that would diminish it as the central force in the Delaware County economy.

CHAPTER III

The Age of Agriculture

Unlike the wilderness of three decades before, Delaware County by the 1850s had become comfortably settled. Dwellings were rarely built of logs any more; sawed lumber was available from several sawmills, and nails and iron products could be obtained from eastern manufacturers (and, by the 1870s, from factories in Muncie). Thus settled, Delaware County began the second half of the 19th century as an agricultural region.

From the 1830s, when the markets were mostly local, to the 1850s, when farmers could sell grain to a mill which in turn could make it into flour and distribute it by railroad or turnpike to other parts of the midwest, agriculture went through a renaissance that continued even past the Civil War.

Delaware County farmers of the 1850s, 1860s, and 1870s directed their efforts toward raising such crops as corn, maize, wheat, oats, barley, and rye. Harvesting was done by hand with much neighborly cooperation. These crops were then marketed locally and resold in milled, distilled, or other processed forms. During this era of agricultural dominance, area industries and commercial firms specialized in serving a rural trade. Blacksmiths and sawmills could be found in Muncie and almost every rural community. In addition, the county seat had slaughterhouses, woolen and cotton mills, knitting works, leather shops, tool manufacturers, and factories that bent and formed wood for tool handles, spokes, wheels, and wagon tops.

Essential to the growth of Delaware County's agricultural trade, however, was good transportation. Thus, from a single "government road" built in the 1820s west from Greenville, Ohio, along White River through Muncie and Anderson, seat of Madison County, by the 1850s Delaware County had a network of roads, built with volunteer labor and contributions, usually along section lines, by which most of the population could be reached and by which farm goods could be carried to market. The first laws providing for gravel roads did not come along until 1858, and when they did, Delaware County stood in good shape: the gravel supply deposited by glaciers thousands of years earlier helped the county get "one up" on other Indiana counties not similarly blessed with this basic material.

The 1860s were patently Delaware County's turnpike years. Numerous privately funded "pikes" were built, connecting towns and farms with one another. Some survived for decades, with tolls furnishing the funds for maintenance after original construction had been financed by subscription.

Some of the turnpikes were the Muncie & Middletown (Henry County), Blountsville (Henry County)—which ran across southeastern Perry Township to Morristown (Randolph County), Range Line Road, Muncie & Wheeling, Middletown & Daleville, Daleville & Bell Creek, Muncie & New Burlington, Muncie & Yorktown, Jackson Street—which ran west from Muncie to the Madison County line, Muncie & Bethel, Muncie & Eaton, Muncie & Granville, Smithfield & Albany, Muncie & Smithfield, Blountsville & Smithfield, Centennial—northeast of Muncie, Mississinewa & Albany, and Mississinewa Valley & New Corner (named for a new settlement in Washington Township).

If a single sociological thread can be discerned from reading a list of the turnpikes, it is that they made it easy (or at least easier) for rural residents of the county to get to Muncie, perhaps spelling the beginning of the end for many rural settlements.

Transportation remained primitive in Delaware County until the first railroad—the Indianapolis & Bellefontaine—came to Muncie in 1852. Several townships voted it cash subsidies. The railroad, which had connections eastward to Cleveland and south from Indianapolis to the Ohio River, offered new routes to larger markets for agricultural products and quicker ways to bring in goods and people.

The age of agriculture saw additional towns platted and developed: New Conner in 1855, Cowan (first called McCowan, after early settler Charles M. McCowan) and Oakville in the 1870s, and Royerton and Shideler with the completion of the Fort Wayne railroad line. DeSoto (first called Woodburn), located in Delaware Township along the railroad, came along to replace Clifton, north along the Mississinewa, and Sharon, just south of Clifton.

In 1848 the state of Indiana had voted to allow public financing of schools, and two years later levies began to be adopted for that purpose. The 1840s had already seen the establishment of Delaware County's Seminary, built by the county in 1841 west of Muncietown—which came to be called Muncie in 1845—on land donated by George W. Garst. (Jefferson School was later built on this site.) Muncie schools were directed by the township trustee until town government was organized in 1855. Under the new town school board, the Seminary was acquired and a steady effort was made, continuing after Muncie became a city in 1865, to improve both the quantity and quality of education. In the 1870s, by the time the city began to acquire a reputation as a commercial center beyond that of just a simple farm marketplace, a high school had been built, and graded classes were being taught in two other buildings to younger pupils. The same kind of school development was also taking place in other county locations, on a smaller scale because of the lack of concentrated population.

Nationally, concern was growing over the rift between slave states in

On January 1, 1860, N.F. Ethell published the first issue of the Delaware County Times. *One of the homes of the paper—which would later be called* The Muncie Times *and then the* Evening Times—*was a brick building near the corner of Main and Walnut streets (right). An advertising card for* The Muncie Times *(far right) dates to about 1883. The daily operation of the* Evening Times *was merged into* The Muncie Evening Press *in the first decade of the 20th century. Engraving from* T.B. Helm, History of Delaware County, Indiana, 1881. *Advertising card courtesy, Mrs. John C. Oesterle*

Right: To finance the building of roads and turnpikes, companies were formed and stock was sold. One, the Muncie & New Burlington Turnpike Company, was formed in the 1870s. From the author's collection

COMPLIMENTS OF

THE MUNCIE TIMES

JOHN F. WILDMAN, Prop.

The Republican Paper of Delaware Co.

SUBSCRIBE NOW. $1 PER YEAR.

BOOK & JOB PRINTING A SPECIALTY.

No. 115   10. 8·6·7 / 25-00 Shares.

The Muncie & New Burlington Turnpike Co.

This Certifies, That *Lazfayette Whitney*
is the owner of *Ten and* 8·6·7 / 25-00 Shares of **TWENTY-FIVE DOLLARS** each, of the
Capital Stock of the Muncie & New Burlington Turnpike Company, of Delaware Co.,
Ind., transferable on the books of said Company, only on the surrender of this Certificate by
said owner, or with his endorsement in blank on the back thereof.

In Witness Whereof, The said Muncie & New Burlington Turnpike Co. has caused the Seal
thereof to be hereunto affixed, and this Certificate to be signed by the President and Secretary
of said Company, this *fourth* day of *June* 1881

M. A. Cunningham President.

Attest: *John Zruck* Secretary.

Fuson Road south of Muncie is named for the family of Delaware Countian Thomas Fuson (above), who served in the 19th Regiment, part of the Iron Brigade, during the Civil War. The regiment's casualties were greater than those suffered by any other Indiana regiment. Fuson saw action at Lookout Mountain, Stone Mountain, Antietam Creek, Second Bull Run, and the Wilderness. After the war Fuson resettled in Delaware County and married a distant relative of Daniel Boone's. Courtesy, Ernest Parkison

Top left: It may have been as late as the 1880s when these members of the Grand Army of the Republic and their families gathered for the photographer. The occasion may have been a reunion of the Iron Brigade. Captain Samuel S. Williams of Selma (a colonel when he was killed in the Wilderness campaign) organized Company K of the Indiana Volunteer Infantry, part of the Iron Brigade. Courtesy, Mick Kissick

Left: Members of the Literary Fireside Society were photographed in a grove of trees in 1886. The organization was one of several cultural groups that developed in post-Civil War years. Courtesy, Jeff Koenker

the south and free states to the north. Because slavery had been barred from the Northwest Territories at their creation in the 1780s, states like Indiana, Ohio, and Illinois, began to attract individuals fleeing slavery.

The effort to smuggle slaves to freedom was greatly supported by some religious groups, and eastern Indiana, with a strong Quaker heritage from Richmond northward, became a favorite, usually safe route for a slave to gain freedom. In the 1850s several farmsteads in eastern Delaware County became "stops" on the Underground Railroad, a system by which fugitive slaves were hidden by day and transported northward by night. Some escaped slaves remained permanently in Delaware County; others passed through on their way to Canada. Free blacks had already come to east central Indiana from western Ohio in the 1840s, settling in Randolph and Delaware counties. Muncie's early black population had these roots. It was not until the 1860s that they had established a number of churches and small businesses in the city.

When the Civil War broke out, Delaware County men comprised more than 23 companies of Union soldiers. Company D of the Eighth Regiment, Indiana Infantry Volunteers, was mustered at Muncie and served at the front at Rich Mountain, Virginia, in an early campaign of General George McClellan's. Plus, the famous Iron Brigade, which included the Nineteenth Indiana Regiment (with companies A, E, and J mustered in Delaware County), took part in such engagements as Gainesville, Second Bull Run, Antietam, and Gettysburg. Colonel Samuel J. Williams of Selma died while leading the Nineteenth in the Battle of the Wilderness in May 1864.

After the war, steady population growth continued in Delaware County. The burgeoning turnpike network was augmented by the construction of the north-south railroad (Connersville & Fort Wayne) and another east-west line (from Sandusky, Ohio, to Lafayette). Mechanization of farm planting and harvesting began.

Two other sources for impetus of town establishment and growth did not occur until later: the final railroad building spree of the late 1890s and early 1900s, and the discovery of natural gas in 1886, which brought upon the county an acceleration in the industrialization that by then was under way. However, although the gas boom is credited for ending the age of agriculture and bringing to Muncie and Delaware County the industrialization which was to dominate the economy for nearly a century, the fact remains that industrialization was already under way when gas was discovered, and agriculture is still a major economic factor in the county nearly a century later.

The proportionate influence of the divergent parts of the economy thus was to change, but not for the reasons often cited, or to the extent many imagine.

CHAPTER IV
Visions of Industry

In 1898 Frank C. Ball patented an automatic glass jar machine that was quickly recognized in the industry as the only practical machine for manufacturing wide-mouth jars and bottles. While hand-blown jars could be produced at the rate of about 10-gross a day by five men in an eight-hour shift, this machine enabled a four-man team to produce 25 gross in the same amount of time, signaling the end of the colorful glassblower's role in commercial production. Glass jar machines were placed around a furnace (in the background) in the Ball Brothers glass plant, shown around the turn of the century. Courtesy, Ball Brothers Foundation

It is oversimplification to date the emergence of Muncie, Delaware County, and east central Indiana as a major industrial area—one that would remain a major industrial area for three-quarters of a century—to the discovery of natural gas. Numerous factors brought visions of industry to Muncie and Delaware County in the years following the Civil War.

The war had caused problems, to be sure, and they did not end when it did. Disabled veterans and dependents of soldiers killed or crippled in action needed assistance. Also, there was an increase of crime, something that accompanies nearly all wartime economies. During the Reconstruction years, Indiana weathered a postwar economic boom, a financial panic, and then a recovery.

Still, Muncie was already on its way toward development as a modern industrial city. In the 1870s a new city hall (Muncie's first, aside from storefront quarters) was constructed. The public library was established in 1874, perhaps encouraged by a realization that education and literacy were important in a faster-moving society. The high school was built in 1880, eliminating the necessity for classes in churches. The city acquired its first steam-powered fire engine in 1874 (although it still had no waterworks to supply its pumps—cisterns under city streets often proved inadequate). And an artificial gasworks (which burned coal to make gas) was put onstream by 1879, allowing the city to brag of its first gas-lit house. In the 1870s and before the gas boom Muncie was slowly beginning to come of age and to move into the mainstream of the industrial revolution.

There was also, after the Civil War, a rising interest in development of the area's natural resources beyond simple cultivation of the topsoil. A geological survey of the state had begun in the 1850s as Hoosiers began to seek out local supplies of coal, gas, and oil. In fact, natural gas had been ignored when first discovered on George Carter's Union Township farm in 1876. The drillers, who were boring for coal, actually feared they had penetrated the reaches of Hell and that the foul-smelling substance which they had tapped was a warning from Lucifer. They capped the well and took their coal-boring crew elsewhere.

Despite all of this growth, a resident of today's Delaware County, conveyed back in time to the Muncie of the mid-1860s, would not have been impressed. The population was somewhere less than 3,000 when city status was achieved in 1865 and John Brady was elected first mayor. Muncie had a two-story brick courthouse (its second, built in the late

Above left: High school students could join sororities and fraternities in the early years of the 20th century, before such organizations were barred in the high schools by Indiana state law. Muncie High School's Kappa Alpha Phi fraternity posed in 1900, dressed to the nines. Courtesy, David M. Meeks

Left: There were at least three country schools along Nebo Road in Mount Pleasant and Harrison townships, including Mount Olive, north of Bethel Pike. This group—meeting for an apparent reunion—are identified as "Boys of Nebo School." Country schools survived into the 20th century despite a consolidation trend that began soon after 1900. Courtesy, E.F. Petty

The National Bank building stands behind this rare scene on Walnut Street north of Main on the east side of the courthouse square. Although the photograph was made in the 1870s, the scene was virtually unchanged from the mid-1850s. The Bacon Clothing Store is at right in a building that dates to the 1830s. Courtesy, Nation-Robinson Printers

1830s) and a few other major buildings, but the streets were of mud and dirt, the sidewalks board, and the houses frame. There was no water or sewage system.

Also, since the county, with a total population perhaps five times that of its seat of government, was developing its turnpike system, these pikes began (or stopped) at the edge of Muncie, so graded roads with scheduled maintenance were something that farmers of Delaware County were to enjoy long before city folk had graded or graveled streets.

Nevertheless, the fact that Muncie was the Delaware County seat and centrally located made it the logical terminus for the turnpikes of the 1860s and 1870s, for the railroads that were built between 1852 and 1901, and later for the electric interurban railroad lines to be built in the early 1900s. Muncie's commercial growth was to accompany all of these developments.

One can probably identify one or two individuals who served as the guiding influence of most small communities during the 19th century and each of its decades. This too was the case with Muncie and Delaware County. Early settlers like Goldsmith C. Gilbert, because of the groundwork they laid, contributed to the eventual enlargement of Muncie as an industrial center. Certainly a key figure in the commercial development of the city was J.W. Burson, who was cashier of the Muncie branch of the Indiana State Bank when the state institution reorganized in 1856, and who continued to be a leading influence in financial circles until his death in 1871. Active in building and civic activities in the 1860s were John Brady, the city's first mayor, and Volney Wilson, a building contractor and entrepreneur. Names like Claypool, Wysor, Andrews, Anthony, Kemper, Marsh, Petty, Spilker, Willard, Kirby, Goddard, and Meeks also figured in Muncie's financial community during the period of slow and then rapid industrialization of the 1870s and 1880s.

The years after the Civil War also brought to Delaware County a man whose reputation as a catalyst and civic booster probably far exceeds that of those who preceded and many who followed him: James Boyce.

James Boyce was no stranger to hardship. At age 12 Boyce was already working 12-hour shifts in a linen factory in his native Ireland, earning eight cents a day. In the 1850s he worked in linen factories in France, and after tiring of this, tried to join the British navy during the Crimean War. Instead, Boyce was talked into shipping to America as a seaman. Boyce arrived in New York to work in a flax mill, and later moved to Ohio for a better position.

In Ohio he went into business for himself; his dam washed away and he went back to work for others. He then went to Minnesota, cleared land and raised flax, alternatively engaging in manufacturing and farming until he acquired a modest estate. Back in Ohio, Boyce co-owned a flax mill that brought him $10,000, the veritable fortune which he took to Muncie in 1870.

Above: General William Harrison Kemper, born in Rush County in 1839 and named for Indiana's first governor, General William (Henry) Harrison, was studying medicine when the Civil War broke out. He was present at 18 battles, returning to Indiana to finish his studies and then practice medicine. He came to Delaware County in 1865. Kemper authored a definitive, two-volume history of Delaware County published in 1908. His two sons, A.T. and W.W. Kemper, also practiced medicine in the county. Courtesy, Ball Memorial Hospital

From the 1890s until 1931 several streetcar routes served Muncie and its burgeoning suburbs of Congerville, Riverside, Industry, Whiteley, Normal City, and Avondale. In the summer, open-air cars were particularly popular on routes going to West Side, Heekin, and McCulloch parks, and residents would ride after dusk just to cool off on hot summer nights. The fare was a nickel. Above right, courtesy, E.F. Petty. Above far right, courtesy, R.A. Greene

Right: The intersection of Main and Walnut streets, viewed looking southeast from the courthouse, was covered with tracks of the new street railways when this photograph was made. At the center of the picture is the Patterson Block, which survives more than a century later. Part of the Willard Block is visible at left, part of Wysor's first Opera House to the right. Courtesy, Ball Stores, Inc.

Soon James Boyce was manufacturing flax bagging and machinery handles. With a work force of 100, he was the city's largest employer. Along with his own commercial enterprises, Boyce—remarkably—was involved in most of the civic improvements made in Muncie during the three decades after his arrival.

James Boyce pushed for the gasworks and municipal sewers, water, and electricity. In 1885 water ran in city water mains for the first time (a franchised company, rather than a municipal utility, installed the system) and the first building was lit with electricity (the Boyce Block). Sewers were underway.

Rumors of gas in Ohio sparked renewed interest in George Carter's 1876 coal-boring incident near Eaton. In 1886 the bore was reopened to the discovery that Delaware County, too, had rich deposits of natural gas.

The supply, residents thought, was limitless. By the end of a year distribution mains were laid in Muncie, and there were seven gas companies serving the county, towns, and countryside. In fact, Muncie bragged that it had no coal or wood yards, because an individual family could get all the fuel it needed as gas for $12 a year. Flambeaux of uncontrolled gas burned brightly at night at wellsites and elsewhere, and there was not much thought given to conservation.

There was thought given to utilization, however. A Board of Trade was formed in 1887, with J.A. Goddard as its president, to sell to the world the merits of locating manufacturing industries in Muncie.

Muncie by the 1880s had something to offer besides cheap fuel. It had made some overtures to culture, it had good transportation (thanks to streets paved early in the decade and the completion of several railroads), and it was early among its peers in getting a telephone system. Furthermore, the center of the population of the United States was gradually drifting westward, so a larger share of the nation's market for industrial goods was moving closer to Delaware County. In 1885 Muncie already boasted factories which produced feather dusters, skewers, tile and brick, spokes, bentwood products, curry combs, reed organs, hubs, wringers, furniture, cigars, boots and shoes, brooms and barrels, food products, and roller skates. (The latter were somehing of a popular phenomenon. Riding the wave of national popularity, Muncie had five skateworks.)

After gas was discovered, the Board of Trade invited new businesses to Muncie, making real estate available at reasonable cost in a community that was obviously willing and able to provide city services. Some 1,400 industrial jobs were created since 1886 at such new firms as Kinnear Manufacturing Company, Brooks Creamery, Ball Brothers Glass Company, G. Jaeger Paper Company, Muncie Rubber Company, Hemingray Glass Company, E.P. Smith and Company, and Thompson Enameling Company. Two of these were major manufacturers that relocated to Muncie: the Ball firm from Buffalo, New York, and the Hemingray firm from Covington, Kentucky.

Right: The cornerstone for Delaware County's third courthouse was laid July 23, 1885. The ornate structure was designed by Brentwood Tolan, a Fort Wayne architect and the son of Ohio native Thomas J. Tolan. Father and son designed numerous buildings in northwestern Ohio and Indiana, including several other Indiana courthouses. This structure was razed in 1966 and 1967, abandoned as impractical because of years of neglect and increased demands for county office space. Photo by Ruth Chin

Left: Muncie's first electric light plant was built at the instigation of James Boyce and others in the 1880s on Wysor Street near Elm and Madison. It was replaced a few years later by a larger plant at Walnut and North streets, the interior of which is shown. Electricity was generated here until the 1930s; by-product steam was piped to heat downtown homes and other buildings. The plant was razed in the 1960s. Courtesy, Jeff Koenker

When the company ran out of warehouse space for glass jars, Ball Brothers resorted to "open storage" in fields near its plants in southeast Muncie (above), shown in 1903. By 1905 the 1,200 workers at the Muncie plant alone were producing 60 million jars a year, to say nothing of plants at other locations in Indiana and Kansas. The five Ball brothers are pictured at about the time they arrived in Muncie (right). Courtesy, Ball Brothers Foundation

Edmund B. Ball

William C. Ball

Lucius L. Ball

Frank C. Ball

George A. Ball

Interest in Muncie as a location for manufacturing firms was affected by two other events of the mid-1880s. A new interstate commerce bill passed by Congress threatened, through railroad rate-making, to paralyze the glass business in the Virginias, giving these companies reason to move to the Gas Belt (although neither Ball nor Hemingray came from the Virginias). Also the 1888 election of Indianapolis lawyer Benjamin Harrison to the Presidency boosted morale in, and focused attention on, the state of Indiana.

One business casualty in the early years of Muncie's gas boom was James Boyce's flax bagging firm, the Muncie Bagging Company. Because the material had to be imported from abroad and the market for flax bags was in the South, Muncie was no longer a feasible location. Boyce was forced to shut down the operation, but remained in Muncie, involved in various real estate and industrial developments.

The city's economic growth continued in the 1890s, spurred by the 1891 creation of the Citizens Enterprise Company, successor of the Board of Trade. Along came a wagon works (it burned but the Enterprise Company collected the insurance), a knitting mill, a gas engine company, and more.

Iron and steel mills took hold. Republic Iron & Steel Company—with its nut and bolt facility—was a Muncie mainstay for several decades. The Midland Steel Company evolved into the huge Inland Steel Corporation which eventually moved to Gary. And when the Whiteley family lost its reaper works to fire, they established a malleable iron foundry in the city. The successor firm, Dayton-Walther Corporation, survives in the 1980s.

Structural steel was a Muncie product beginning at gas boom times with the locally organized Indiana Bridge Company producing structural steel for buildings and the hundreds of steel bridges built along Midwestern roads in the 1880s and 1890s.

The era of industrialization and its improvements in transportation and communication, which followed increased interest in education, also brought to the area—and to Muncie in particular—a fascination with music, art, and literature beyond what the schools and public library could provide. Muncie residents in the final years of the 19th century established an Art Students League, a Ladies' Matinee Musicale, and a literary club—the MacRae—which all remain active nearly a century later. Various lodges for women, the Muncie Art Association, and any number of other philanthropic clubs and societies came along in the same era.

Obviously such organizations existed because a growing population could support them. Muncie nearly doubled its population from 1870 to 1880, from 2,892 to 5,219. By 1890, thanks to the impetus brought by the rediscovery of natural gas, the population did double to 11,345. Despite the depletion of the cheap gas supply, industry still grew, and in 1900

Top right: The Kitselman brothers came to Muncie from Ridgeville, in Randolph County, to manufacture their patented fence-making machinery. The "Duplex" machine was used to construct fence material in the field. Courtesy, James Wingate

Top far right: A view of White River east of Muncie, seen from near Ball Road and Gavin Avenue, shows two steel bridges that may have been manufactured by Indiana Bridge Company, founded in Muncie in the late 1880s. The bridge in the foreground was for street traffic, while the one in background carried interurban cars on a line that ran east to Selma, Winchester, and Union City. From the author's collection

Center: The firm of Busch and Russell provided monuments and headstones to Delaware County customers around the turn of the century. It also provided building stone for residential and commercial construction. The office and yard shown were on Kilgore Avenue opposite Beech Grove Cemetery. Courtesy, Ball Brothers Foundation

Bottom right: These young ladies and gentlemen, pictured around 1910 in front of the home of pioneer New Burlington physician Dr. Samuel Jump, may have been members of a Sunday School class at the New Burlington Methodist Church. Courtesy, Rita Winters

Bottom far right: White was fashionable for tennis even then, but the men wore neckties and the ladies long dresses when this photograph was taken on the courts of Eastern Indiana Normal University, perhaps as early as the turn of the century. The clay courts were located behind the school's main building— now remodeled many times over—the administration building of Ball State University. Courtesy, E.F. Petty

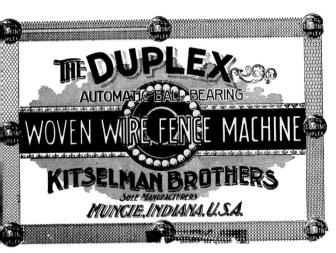

Right: Equipment in Muncie's three fire stations was completly motorized prior to World War I, although a large steam fire engine was kept in reserve at the downtown station and used as late as 1918. Shown are the men of Station Three, Council and Willard streets, with their combination pumper and hose truck, one of Muncie's first motorized fire engines. The station was razed in the mid-1960s after a new, larger one was built nearby. Courtesy, R.A. Greene

Left: The turn-of-the-century White & Haymond law office in Muncie at first glance seems typical. Not so typical are the two telephones in the background: the community had two competing telephone systems for more than two decades, and businesses and professionals usually subscribed to both. Lawyers of the era, like physicians of several decades earlier, were often not college-educated but had "read" under the guidance of a senior practitioner. Courtesy, Beasley & Gilkison

Below: Thomas P. Kirby, a plumber with offices in the 100 block of East Main Street, was photographed in the 1890s with his employees in front of his shop. Courtesy, Jeff Koenker

Muncie had 20, 942 residents. In 1910, when the gas boom momentum was finally gone for good, Muncie's population was 24,005.

And the gas did run out. In 1901, there was a near panic when pressure failed in the lines of the Muncie Natural Gas Company and the Heat, Light and Power Company. The city council appointed a committee to investigate. There was even talk of reviving the artificial gasworks of the 1870s and 1880s, which had burned coal to make gas before plentiful natural gas had been found.

Although the gas supply would dwindle, the base of Muncie as a manufacturing center had been established. Further westward movement in the nation's population brought markets closer to Muncie. Two more railroads hauled in coal and hauled out glass and steel products. And on the horizon came an invention that was to change the face of the nation as a whole: the automobile. One was on display at the 1895 Columbian Exposition in Chicago, and Elwood Haynes, a young man from Portland, about 30 miles from Muncie, was already using one he had built for his work—supervising and maintaining Jay County's natural gas system, a job which required a lot of rural travel.

If the presence of natural gas made a city out of Muncie, then the industries relating to the production of the automobile kept Muncie one. Because of the automobile industry Muncie would be an industrial center for more than 50 more years, natural gas, steel, and glass notwithstanding. Muncie moved into the 20th century.

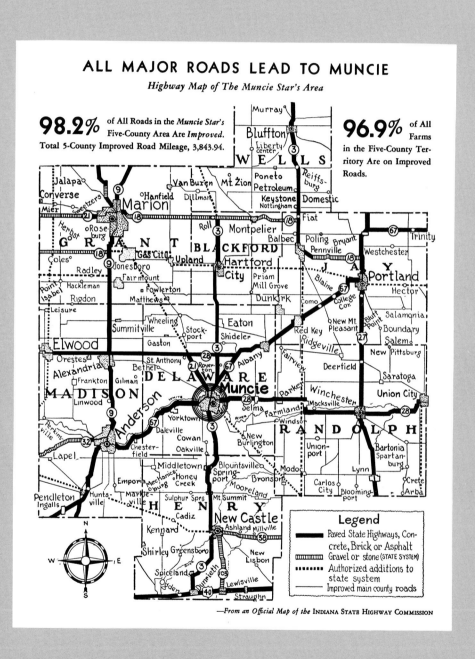

ALL MAJOR ROADS LEAD TO MUNCIE

Highway Map of The Muncie Star's Area

98.2% of All Roads in the *Muncie Star's* Five-County Area Are *Improved.* Total 5-County Improved Road Mileage, 3,843.94.

96.9% of All Farms in the Five-County Territory Are on Improved Roads.

—*From an Official Map of the* INDIANA STATE HIGHWAY COMMISSION

Motorcars and Rapid Change

Muncie of the early 1900s was a thriving city. Its industrial base had survived the nation's Panic of 1893 as well as the diminishment of the local "endless" supply of natural gas.

Muncie's development brought on growth in city services. A city controller's report issued in 1907 lists three fire stations and 20 paid fire-fighters. The same report tells of the city burning its garbage—including stray domestic animals—in a city "crematory" or incinerator, located at 18th and Hackley streets on the far south side. The police department of the day boasted a horse, a patrol wagon, and three bicycles. The city also had a contract with the husband-and-wife team of Drs. W.D. and E.A. Whitney for its first hospital in their combination home and office near downtown. Moreover, the city engineer in 1907 proudly pointed to Muncie's 60 miles of paved streets (out of a total of 75 miles), a far cry from the dusty, muddy streets of a quarter-century before. Sewers had been extended, although they would continue to dump untreated waste into White River well into the 1930s.

Delaware County's incorporated towns were also prospering as the 20th century began. Gaston, founded as New Corner in the middle of the 19th century, was given new life when the Cincinnati, Richmond & Muncie Railroad arrived. Albany, which dated to the 1830s, grew slowly throughout its existence thanks to the new railroad in the 1880s and the interurban after 1900. Yorktown, also an old community, benefited from some gas boom industrialization, while Eaton, the county's third largest community behind Muncie and Albany, had (and profited from having) the county's first operating gas well. Selma, a creature of the Bee Line Railroad of 1852, was the site—with neighboring Smithfield, now barely a hamlet—of an oil boom in the 1890s following the gas boom of the decade before. Finally, some of Albany's citizens, led by J.D. Manor, put together a development effort much like Muncie's successful Citizens Enterprise Company, attracting a paper mill, glassworks, furniture factory, china factory, and other firms. A fire department was organized, gas and electric lines were installed, and at one time in the decade some 150 houses were reported under construction. The other town, Normal City, was a new one created around the campus of the new normal school. It also attracted some industry at its edges, for example, a bending works and a paper mill. Normal City did not survive long as a corporation, being absorbed, like its immediate and newer neighbor Riverside, into Muncie a few years later.

Top left: Lake Erie & Western Railway workers pose beside a locomotive in the Muncie yards early in the century. The donkey may have just been transportation for yard conductor "Dode" Thorpe. At left are yard helpers Rex Moler and "Scary" Quirk, and engineer Leroy (Paddy) Dole; at right is fireman John Stamm. The locomotive was built in 1893, acquired by the LE&W in 1905, and scrapped in 1922. Courtesy, R.A. Greene

Top right: In 1901 the Cincinnati, Richmond, and Muncie Railroad completed its tracks to Muncie. This passenger station at Wysor and Vine streets was dedicated in 1902, and it still served the railroad's successor, the Chesapeake and Ohio Railroad, 80 years later. Muncie's industrial development in the 1880s and 1890s made the city a desirable target for railroad construction. From the author's collection

Above: For four decades until the line was abandoned in 1941, the interurban tracks connecting Muncie with Anderson and Indianapolis traversed Yorktown's Smith Street through the business district. Most of the buildings shown were still there some six decades later. The photograph was probably made around 1920. From the Swift collection. Courtesy, Ball State University

Left: On March 25, 1913, residents of North Elm Street ventured forth to find their neighborhood flooded from nearby White River in the worst flood ever recorded in the central Midwest. A scene in Riverside shows University Avenue from Pauline Avenue. Floodwaters that rose throughout the Midwest in March of 1913 were particularly disastrous to the nation's largest railroad, the Pennsylvania Railroad, because it had so much property in the Ohio River Valley. The Pittsburgh, Columbus, Chicago & St. Louis, a PRR subsidiary that served Muncie, sustained heavy damage as its yards along North Madison Street were inundated. From the author's collection

Below: The main street of Selma, photographed sometime in the early 1920s, was populated by two automobiles, two horse-and-wagon outfits, and three pedestrians. Selma, which grew up in the 1850s after the railroad came, was an oil-and-gas-boom town in the last part of the 19th century. Its population shrank to about 400 by 1930, after which time it has grown as a "suburb" of Muncie. From the Swift collection. Courtesy, Ball State University

Dr. William Mix (top) and Dr. George Andrews (above, with glasses) were partners in a hospital in downtown Muncie in the early years of the century. Dr. Andrews later founded Muncie Home Hospital, a much larger facility south of the business district. Drs. Mix and Andrews both practiced at Home Hospital. Courtesy, Ball Memorial Hospital

If the name of James Boyce stands out as the human lever behind the development of Muncie into a city in the 1870s and 1880s, two other names stand out as key to Muncie's continued development prior to the end of the 19th century: Ball and McCulloch.

Five brothers from New York state—Lucius L., William C., Edmund B., Frank C., and George A. Ball—who had brought their glass manufacturing plant to Muncie soon after the Gas Boom of the late 1880s began—were in Muncie to stay as the 20th century began.

And also in the 1880s, a young lawyer named George McCulloch was beginning to be known locally. Born in Ohio and raised in Muncie, McCulloch engaged in several small business enterprises before becoming deputy county clerk in the 1870s. He practiced law briefly, served for two terms as county clerk and then was secretary of the Citizens Enterprise Company.

George McCulloch is credited with resuscitating and electrifying the city's tired street railway and with developing electric interurban lines connecting Muncie to the seats of five of the seven adjacent counties, as well as to Indianapolis, Fort Wayne, Dayton, and other Midwestern urban centers. Also, in 1899 he established *The Muncie Morning Star*, a daily newspaper which was distributed throughout central and eastern Indiana and which helped identify Muncie to its wide readership as a retail and commercial center.

So far, the automobile had not become significant to the county or the nation as a whole. Railroads were still the primary means of transport into the early 20th century. The Cincinnati, Richmond & Muncie (now the Chesapeake & Ohio) was completed into Muncie in 1903, and by 1907 the whole line from Cincinnati to Chicago was operable. The Chicago, Indiana & Eastern, completed into Muncie from Miami and Grant counties in 1900, eventually was acquired by a subsidiary of the giant Pennsylvania Railroad system, giving the PRR a competetive edge in the shipment of Muncie's glass and steel products. A third railroad latecomer was the Chicago & Southeastern (also called the Indiana Midland or Central Indiana). The heyday of American steam railroads was the first 20 years of the 20th century; since then, abandonment of railroad lines has almost always exceeded new construction.

The first 20 years of the century were also the years of Indiana's (and other states') interurban railroads. Thus Muncie got, prior to World War I, an interurban terminal at Charles and Mulberry streets that had a two-story office building, a separate freighthouse, and a covered trainshed with four tracks. Under the terminal's steel roof, electric cars arrived from and departed for points throughout Delaware County and Indiana, plus cities including Waterloo, Iowa, Louisville, Kentucky, and Dayton, Ohio. By making it easy to get to Muncie, the interurbans did in the first two decades of the century what the steam railroads had done beginning after the Civil War and what the automobile would do later: diminish the importance of smaller, rural communities.

As Muncie and Delaware County grew, communication and higher education became increasingly important. Telephone service was established in the county as early as 1880 and was in widespread use by 1890. The first decade of the 20th century saw the founding of the second of the city's two surviving newspapers, the *Muncie Evening Press*, in 1905. It survives with *The Muncie Star* (the word "morning" was dropped in the 1940s) under common ownership that also dates to the mid-1940s.

In the early 1890s private normal schools began to be established in various parts of the country. These schools offered not only post high school courses but, for those whose communities did not have them, high school courses for boarding students. They also offered teacher training, something that in the 1870s and 1880s was mainly handled in brief summer institutes in county seat communities. As early as 1893 a Muncie native living in Fort Scott, Kansas, wrote to his brother to suggest that Muncie would be the logical site for a normal school. It would be prestigious, he noted, and would stimulate trade; at least that was the effect that such a school had had on Fort Scott.

The year 1896 saw the incorporation of the Eastern Indiana Normal University. The corporation purchased undeveloped land on the west side of Muncie across White River, a mile from the courthouse. Proceeds from the land's sale were to be used to construct the university facility. The first lots did not sell quickly, but by 1898 finally some 300 lots were sold at $300 apiece. The $90,000 thus raised built a three-story brick and stone structure in a former cornfield on Muncie's west side, and Eastern Indiana Normal University became a reality. The building was the forerunner, as was the university it housed, of the present Ball State University. It stands, remodeled numerous times, as the university's current administration building.

Muncie attracted a second institution of higher learning a few years later. In 1908 a Muncie branch of the Indiana Business College opened, and it has remained in operation continuously since that time.

However, Eastern Indiana Normal University did not fare as well with regard to operating continuity. The school opened in the fall of 1899 in its new town, Normal City, which the developers hoped would succeed as a residential suburb of Muncie. The town developed slowly, the university falteringly. After two years the school closed, and in the following 17 years three other private educational institutions were attempted on the campus. None could make the financial grade. In fact, the Muncie Commercial Club—predecessor of the Muncie-Delaware County Chamber of Commerce—published a brochure in the early 1910s touting the campus as the future site of the International School of Hotel Management. That school, in fact, located with Cornell University in Ithaca, New York.

The campus was vacant in 1918 when the Ball brothers bought the

The Columbia Theatre

OPENS MONDAY
SEPTEMBER 1, 1913

WITH MOTION PICTURES DELUX

THE Motion Picture Show places have become a fixed institution in this country. They have found a permanent place as American enterprises and are here to stay. Recognizing this fact, the HOME MOTION PICTURE COMPANY has erected a beautiful, modern and costly theatre, at 310 S. Walnut street, in which moving pictures of the very highest class will be shown. Nothing has been left undone in the construction and arrangement of this magnificent theatre to give to its patrons every convenience and comfort that modern science can invent.

SOME IMPORTANT FEATURES FOR YOUR COMFORT AND PLEASURE AT THE COLUMBIA THEATRE

No finer program of motion pictures will be shown anywhere. Our library is replete with comedies, dramas, educational, scientific and scenic subjects.

Our indirect lighting system is the finest ever.

Positively the most modern ventilating and sanitary systems to be obtained have been installed in this theatre.

Our pipe organ is the acme of perfection in construction and harmonious melody.

Don't let anything spoil your arrangements to visit

"THE HOUSE OF QUALITY"
ON THE OPENING DATE, MONDAY SEPT. 1, at 1 O'CLOCK P. M.

IN REGARD TO OUR INDIRECT LIGHTING SYSTEM

ENDORSED BY THE PULPIT   COMMENDED BY THE PRESS
AND DEMANDED BY THE PUBLIC

Indirect illumination is a tremendous asset to motion pictures.

Its use eliminates characters who seek dark corners.

It lights the theatre in the only way that relieves the eyestrain.

It beautifies, enlarges and gives a hygenic appearance, all of which are impossible with any direct lighting scheme.

The indirect lighting system will be appreciated by all of our patrons who go to their seats *without groping blindly* down the aisle, *stumbling over* and otherwise *disturbing others* in the audience, as was the case in the "dark ages."

You can go directly from the box office to vacant seats without falling all over other people--without being blinded by darkness.

You can enjoy the pictures in a manner impossible in a dark house, as there is no vivid contrast between the bright screen and the surrounding inky blackness.

"THE HOUSE OF QUALITY"
WILL OPEN MONDAY, SEPTEMBER 1, 1913
AT 1 O'CLOCK P. M.

Central Printing Co. Muncie, Indiana

Muncie's Columbia Theatre opened on September 1, 1913, in the 300 block of South Walnut Street. The theater thrived for more than a decade until the larger Rivoli Theatre, a block away, replaced it as the city's most modern, and until "talkies" replaced the silent films. From the author's collection

Top: Men with a team prepare to erect a pole for lighting an athletic field near Wysor and Walnut streets in Muncie, perhaps about the time of World War I. McKinley School, razed in the 1970s, can be seen in the background. The site later would be occupied by the schools' fieldhouse (late 1920s) and McKinley Junior High School (mid-1930s). Courtesy, Jeff Koenker

Above: Telephone operators stand at their posts in the Indiana Bell exchange at 215 East Jackson Street. The system was automated in the late 1930s along with exchanges in Yorktown, Albany, and Eaton. The long-distance switchboard remained in this building—which was razed in the 1970s—well into the 1950s. From the Swift collection. Courtesy, Ball State University

Right: The days of the former Riverside School in the recently annexed Muncie westside suburb were numbered when this picture was taken in 1923; the new Emerson school had already been erected behind it. By the mid-1980s Emerson, too, is gone: the neighborhood between downtown and Ball State had changed from an area of families to one dominated by single university students. Courtesy, Jeff Koenker

Right: First graders at Garfield Elementary School in Muncie pose for a photograph with their teacher in 1907 or 1908. From the author's collection

property and donated it to the state of Indiana, which reopened the school as the eastern branch of Indiana State Normal School, then located at Terre Haute. Later the Muncie campus became an independent entity, Ball State Teachers College, in 1929. The Balls donated generously to its capital expansion in the 1920s and 1930s and continue to be among its major benefactors.

Into the 20th century, formal education in the rest of the country improved as well. Rural schools—often two- or four-room schools, depending upon the resources of the community—were shut down and children hauled by horse hack (later by bus) to centrally located schools in nearby towns or townships. Early consolidated schools often were expanded town schools, since teachers could find lodging more easily in a town than in a rural area. Frequently, services like water and fire protection served as added inducements for schools to consolidate "in town."

Unincorporated communities also were consolidation focal points, Salem Township schools being consolidated into a school in Daleville, Monroe Township's (including Oakville's) into Cowan because of its central location, Hamilton Township's into Royerton, and Delaware Township's into DeSoto. Only two townships boasted strictly rural consolidated schools: Perry Township, where the Center School was enlarged because of its central location, and Harrison Township, where a new consolidated school was finally built after World War I.

As demand for better educational facilities grew, so did the need for an expanded public library. Although Muncie boasted a public library (located in a room in City Hall at Jackson and Jefferson streets) long before the gas boom, the facility was thought inadequate by many, and in 1901 a citizens committee of the Commercial Club, Hardin Rhoads, James A. Daly, and J.C. Johnson, wrote asking philanthropist Andrew Carnegie to support a library project in Muncie. The response was that if Muncie residents would agree to spend $5,000 a year to support a public library, Carnegie would donate $50,000 toward its construction. The city council quickly accepted the offer and purchased the corner property southeast of city hall for $13,000. (A property previously given to the city for library purposes was sold for $6,000, making the net land cost $7,000.) On January 1, 1904, the new Muncie Public Library was dedicated. The same building still serves as the library's main branch.

The rapid development of the automobile from a tinkerer's toy to a vehicle of commercial and social use changed Muncie as an industrial center. Although Muncie still made glass and other products into the early 1960s, it started, prior to World War I, to manufacture automobiles, automobile parts, and other automobile-related machinery.

During this period of expansion and prosperity, local firms proliferated. Parts made in Muncie ranged from auto tops to wheels; vehicles included tractors and potato diggers as well as such automobiles

Right: Employees of the T.W. Warner Company, a maker of automobile parts, gathered for this group picture in front of the plant at Kilgore and Perkins avenues (later the Muncie Trade School), perhaps around the time of World War I. Courtesy, Fred Lewis family

A few years after he founded General Motors, W.G. Durant left that firm and with several others founded Durant Motors. He acquired the former Sheridan auto factory in Muncie and there manufactured cars under the Durant and Star names. Below right: A Durant automobile sits in front of the factory in Muncie where it was manufactured. Below far right: The Durant Motors four-cylinder Star touring car, also photographed in front of its Muncie factory, was one of the most popular built by the firm. The Muncie factory building became the General Motors Delco-Remy battery plant later in the 1920s, and in the late 1970s, when the battery plant moved to another Muncie location, the site was taken over by an expanding General Motors (Chevrolet) transmission plant. From the Swift collection. Courtesy, Ball State University

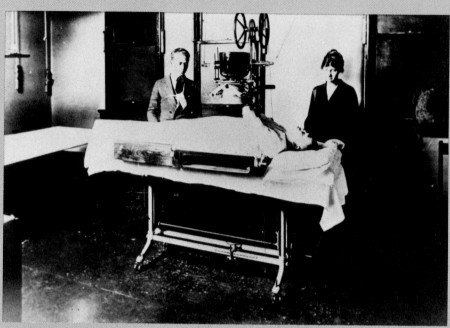

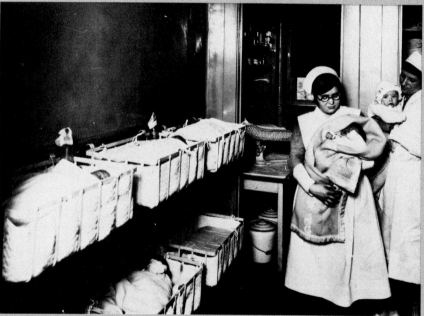

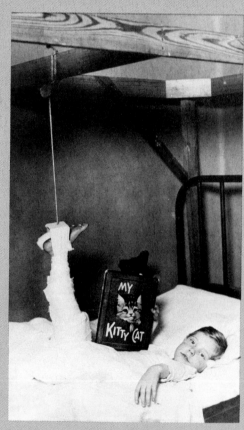

Top left: Dr. Clay A. Ball practiced medicine in Muncie for 68 years before his death in 1980. He was associated with three hospitals: one operated by Drs. William Mix and George Andrews; the Home Hospital, which Andrews helped start; and Ball Memorial Hospital, completed in 1929. However, most of his practice was carried on in his office or at patients' homes. He rode streetcars and rented livery buggies to reach his patients before getting his first car in 1914. Dr. Ball is pictured in 1977. Courtesy, The Muncie Star

Muncie Home Hospital, founded around 1913, was Delaware County's most up-to-date medical facility until Ball Memorial Hospital replaced it in 1929. Left: A wooden frame provides the right angle for traction of a young Home Hospital patient's broken leg. Far left: Although the trend toward giving birth in hospitals had barely begun in Delaware County, the hospital's newborn nursery seems to be overpopulated in this mid-1920s photograph. Above left: Home Hospital's early X-ray equipment was simple almost to the point of being spartan. The X-ray device is on the machine above the patient; the film is beneath him on the table; and neither attendant wears any protective garb. Above: A class of nurses-in-training poses at Home Hospital. The nursing school moved to Ball Memorial Hospital when the new facility opened in 1929, and was operated there until the 1960s, when baccalaureate-degree nursing courses were moved to Ball State University in cooperation with the hospital. Nursery photo from the Swift collection; courtesy, Ball State University. Other photos courtesy, Ball Memorial Hospital

Left: The Muncie Home Guards assembled during World War I, although they did not serve overseas. Delaware County's soldiers who did participate were members of Company L, Third Infantry, Indiana State Militia. Photo by Otto Sellers. From Lannes McPhetridge, Delaware County in the World War, 1919

Above left: The greatest Labor Day demonstration that Muncie had ever seen— "Win the War Day"— took place on September 2, 1918. An army of industrial workers paraded with banners, flags, and floats, many showing a particular company's contribution to the war effort. Women workers from Ontario Silver Company—which made soldiers' mess table equipment, knives, forks, and spoons— pose in the company's Labor Day float. Photo by Otto Sellers. From Lannes McPhetridge, Delaware County in the World War, 1919

Above: As Muncie moved from wartime years to the Roaring Twenties, many urban storefront restaurants of the period looked very much like Payne's Cafe on East Main Street. Payne's Cafe vied— successfully—with the Braun Hotel as the place to dine out in east central Indiana. Patrons could make their way from other cities and towns to the restaurant via automobile, streetcar, and interurban. The cafe operated until the late 1950s. From the Swift collection. Courtesy, Ball State University

Ball Gymnasium, Lucina Hall, and the library on campus, and Home Hospital was replaced by the larger, more modern Ball Memorial Hospital. Organized athletics at the high school level began before World War I and continued to grow in the 1920s; basketball successes and growing interest in the sport led to the city school's construction in the late 1920s of the largest high school fieldhouse in the nation, with a spectator area seating more than 7,500 people.

Prohibition, which followed quickly on the heels of the World War I armistice, closed down Muncie's one brewery, and the production of alcohol was driven underground. Speakeasies existed throughout the city and county, and the increasing mobility of the population, a larger proportion each year owning motorcars, made enforcement difficult. The social experiment may have contributed to a rising crime rate in the city, but it may be more accurate to blame increased crime on the increased mobility of the population and the unsettling influence of the war. America's "Public Enemy Number One," wanted for murder in Connecticut and escaping from the federal penitentiary in Atlanta, Gerald Chapman came to the Muncie area in late 1924. He was captured by four city police officers in January of 1925.

Aside from Prohibition, the other constitutional amendment that would affect social patterns in the 1920s was women's suffrage. Women gained not only the vote, but also access to professions such as law and journalism.

After the war one of the most significant of the area's events was sociologist Robert S. Lynd's choosing Muncie for a major study. Lynd wanted to show how 30 years of accelerated industrialization in the nation had changed people's values and priorities, especially with regard to religion. Lynd and his wife Helen Merrell Lynd lived in Muncie during the year-long study. Their findings were published in 1929 as *Middletown*, a volume which quickly became standard reading for would-be sociologists and much of the American public.

Lynd later said he chose the city because of its size (he needed a place where a significant sample could be polled or interviewed), its lack of a dominating ethnic group or "first family," and its lack of any major influential educational institution. When he returned in the 1930s to study how the community had fared during the Depression, he corrected perceived errors with regard to the influence of the Ball family, which had lent the city some financial stability during nationwide bank failures. In the new study, *Middletown in Transition*, the college's influence in the community was considerably greater than before, perhaps to the extent that he would not have chosen Muncie for the initial study had he been doing it in the mid-1930s.

Through the two studies Muncie gained some notoriety nationwide as "typical America." This reputation has been seized upon both by promoters of Muncie's business and commercial growth and by

Right: The automobile made it possible for the Muncie Public Library in the 1920s to take its services from neighborhood to neighborhood. An early bookmobile is shown in a city park—perhaps Heekin Park where the first branch library building, the Grace Keiser Maring branch, was constructed in the 1930s. Courtesy, E.F. Petty

Below right: The Muncie Malleable Foundry provides the backdrop for this picture of a Muncie High School football team, taken in McCulloch Park in the late 1920s. Coach Walter Fisher is at right, assistant coach Norman Durham at left. From the Swift collection. Courtesy, Ball State University

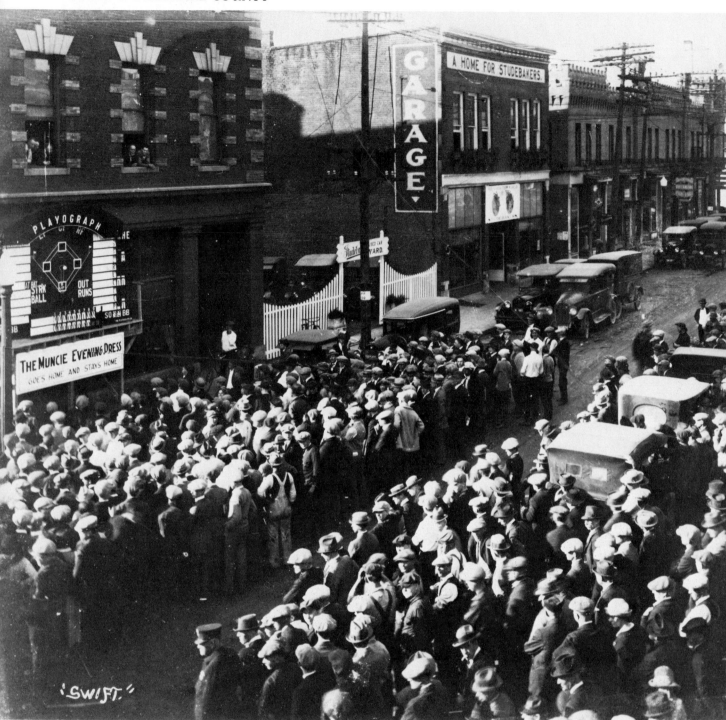

Above: Vehicles were double-parked and people stood in the street (in the pre-radio days of the mid-1920s) to "watch" the World Series on a "Playograph" board set up in front of the office of the Muncie Evening Press. *The paper— still located at 125 South High Street—received scores and play-by-play information by telegraph from the stadium and placed the information on the board. From the Swift collection. Courtesy, Ball State University*

Left: A "Rest Room" at the Delaware County Fair in the 1920s meant a place to rest—and perhaps look at some latest fashions. From the Swift collection. Courtesy, Ball State University

Left: A bearded, sooty Santa Claus shunned Donder and Blitzen to arrive in Muncie by airplane at least once prior to 1930. Surrounded by onlookers, the rather large elf and, presumably, his pilot are shown getting out of a two-seater at the Wall Airport on Hackley Street south of 18th Street. The airport was displaced in the early 1930s by a newer field north of the city. From the Swift collection. Courtesy, Ball State University

Above: The Knights Templar of Muncie Commandery 18, were in full regalia when they posed in the 100 block of South Franklin Street, probably in the 1920s. The group was one of numerous Masonic organizations that traced their Delaware County heritage back to the middle of the 19th century. From the Swift collection. Courtesy, Ball State University

Left: This 1920s dental laboratory in Muncie's Johnson Block seems primitive by today's standards. From the Swift collection. Courtesy, Ball State University

Far left: The Delaware County National Bank, founded in 1887, was nearly 50 years old when it moved next door into this new building (shown while still under construction) in 1926, giving up quarters in the Willard Block. In the bank reorganizations of the 1930s, the Merchants Trust and Savings Corporation, a state bank, succeeded the Delaware County National Bank. In the late 1950s a federal charter was issued and the name changed to American National Bank and Trust Company, which still maintains its main office in the 110 East Main Street building. From the Swift collection. Courtesy, Ball State University

Left: Workers at the French Steam Dye Works, in the 400 block of East Main Street, paused to be photographed in the mid-1920s. Hand-pressing was apparently a specialty of the dry cleaning shop. From the Swift collection. Courtesy, Ball State University

researchers using the huge amounts of baseline data or seeking "typical America's" reactions and opinions.

The prosperous times of the 1920s were replaced by the worst economic depression of the nation in the early 1930s. In Delaware County employment slumped, businesses failed, and relief rolls grew. The community gained some economic stability from construction at the young teachers' college. Additional buildings added in the late 1930s were mostly benefactions of the Ball family, although one, the Fine Arts building, was partially federally funded. Residential construction also rebounded slowly, and some factory space was added in the middle and late 1930s. The city built McKinley Junior High School; Ball State doubled the size of Burris Laboratory School. The Ball family also added the E.B. Ball Medical Building to Ball Memorial Hospital. A nurses' dormitory, Maria Bingham Hall, had been completed earlier in the decade.

Federally funded public works projects also provided employment to area residents during the Depression. Projects in Muncie included the grade separation on South Madison Street, five bridges over White River, Munsyana Homes—the county's first subsidized housing project—and vastly improved sewers along with a treatment plant west of the city. White River, long a receptacle of raw sewage and industrial waste, was finally being cleaned up.

When the United States entered World War II in 1941, many of Muncie's industries were already involved in war production. Lifestyles changed to an even greater extent than they had in World War I. Hundreds of women poured into the work force—many to remain permanently—as men enlisted or were drafted. Gasoline, tires, shoes, canned goods and dairy products were rationed, and blackouts (for fear) and brownouts (for conservation) darkened the county for five years.

In addition, training programs for Navy fliers were in operation at Ball State Teachers College and at the Muncie Aviation Company, the airport which had grown to maturity north of the city on Center Pike in the previous 10 years.

The war's end saw residents of Muncie and Delaware County starved for consumer goods of all description. A boom in housing stemmed from World War II marriages and new families created thereby, and educational allowances voted veterans by the Congress brought new growth to Ball State Teachers College. Muncie and Delaware County were at the halfway mark, chronologically, in the 20th century.

Left: Soon after Middletown in Transition, Robert Lynd's second sociological survey of Muncie, appeared in the mid-1930s, the new Life Magazine sent photojournalist Margaret Bourke White to Muncie. Miss White was herself photographed with city officials in the council chambers of City Hall. Her pictures of people were thought by many local residents to be unflattering and demeaning. Courtesy, William O. Shroyer

Above left: A desolate wintry view of the Big Four Railroad yards in Muncie was taken in the middle 1930s, looking east from Walnut Street just south of Union Station. Photo by R.A. Greene. From the author's collection

Above far left: Dedication ceremonies were conducted in 1937 for the Daniel Chester French statue Beneficence, a monument to the philanthropy of the five Ball brothers from the citizens of Muncie. The statue was erected on the campus of Ball State Teachers College seven years after it was commissioned: raising the money for the monument was difficult in the Depression years. The statue stands at the north end of Talley Avenue. Courtesy, Robert L. Barnet

Above: An aerial view looking southwest over Blaine School shows the huge Ball Brothers glass factories in southeast Muncie probably in the early or mid-1930s. At the top right of the photo is Heekin Park—residential areas to the park's south were not built up until after World War II. The former Hemingray Glass plant, acquired by Owens Illinois in early 1930s, is at left. Glass manufacturing stopped at the Ball plant in 1962, but other functions are carried out there two decades later; the O-I complex was turned into warehousing later in 1960s. Courtesy, Ball Brothers Foundation

Delaware County had begun to outgrow Muncie's Home Hospital by the late 1920s. Because of its location in a crowded area near downtown, the hospital itself could not expand sufficiently to meet the community's needs. The Ball family came through to donate a new, modern facility to the area. Above: Members of the Ball families and others were on hand on June 7, 1927, when ground was broken for Ball Memorial Hospital. The site was west of the Ball State Teachers College campus in an area that once had a country club and golf course nearly two decades earlier. Construction would take two years. Left: Prior to the opening of Ball Memorial Hospital in 1929, most babies in Delaware County were born at home. Charles Edwin Nelson, born at 2:05 p.m. on August 8, 1929, was the first child born in the new medical facility. Opposite page, top left: Ball Memorial Hospital, when it opened, was self-sufficient with regard to laundry facilities. Hospital laundry employees of the 1920s are shown in the laundry and storage building to the rear of the main hospital, running linen through a huge commercial mangle. Opposite page, bottom: Nursing students, nurses, doctors, and staff from Ball Memorial Hospital assembled, along with townspeople and photographer Otto Sellers,

at the 1935 groundbreaking for the Edmund Burke Ball Medical Building southwest of the main hospital building pictured. The new building was to contain additional space for patients, X-ray and laboratory facilities, and classrooms. It was the fourth building in Muncie's medical center complex next to Ball State. Top right: When a poliomyelitis epidemic swept the Midwest in the summer of 1949, hospitals ran short of iron lungs for patients with breathing problems. Nellie Brown, Ball Memorial Hospital superintendent, and Jack Reichart, an inventor and president of Muncie's Excel Manufacturing Company, pooled their knowledge to build several iron lungs locally to Reichart's design, using oil drums for the body of the lung. Reichart is shown with one of the iron lungs. Photos courtesy, Ball Memorial Hospital

CHAPTER VI

Mid-century Readjustments

Although Muncie's fire chief had enjoyed a closed car (far left) for several years, the first fire trucks with covered cabs were not acquired by the city until 1943, when a pumper (left) and an aerial ladder truck (right) were purchased to replace similar outdated equipment. The modern equipment is shown at Central Fire Station along with a 1928 pumper (far right). Courtesy, James R. Bailey

Although consumer goods that had been rationed or in short supply during World War II were again available, Muncie and Delaware County entered the second half of the 20th century preoccupied with shortages. Building contractors were scrambling for materials to construct residential housing for a growing population of returned GIs and their families—families producing children who would need to be fitted into the already-crowded school system. The crowded hospital barely resembled the commodious building of the early 1930s. A shortage of physicians during the war years had brought citizens to Ball Memorial Hospital for basic as well as major or emergency medical care, and returning servicemen reinforced and accelerated the trend. As the birth rate climbed and as medical science advanced, by mid-century beds lined even the hospital's sunrooms and corridors.

These shortages were brought on, in many ways, by postwar growth. Residential areas sprang up in numerous locations in and around Muncie—fields that were used as baseball lots by local kids and for "victory gardens" during the war were soon hard to find. Nevertheless, much of Delaware County was still, at the midpoint of the 20th century, basically rural. Smaller county communities, while growing, did not grow at as fast a pace as Muncie, and within the county's nearly 400 square miles Muncie and the five other incorporated towns covered less than 10 square miles. Town or city residents wanted to live within walking distance of schools, stores, and churches. Suburban residential developments outside any municipal corporation were rare; non-adjacent ones were virtually non-existent.

The middle years of the 20th century saw shifts in farming economics in Delaware County, reflecting those elsewhere in the state and nation. The 1930s had seen the beginning of the trend in which owners of small farms sought employment in town and city shops and factories, first to augment their incomes and then, in the 1940s, to assist the war effort. After the war many returning servicemen went to college on the GI Bill of Rights, further drying up the pool of available manpower for farms. In order to stay competitive and solvent, family farms tended, therefore, to grow, mechanize, and specialize in raising a single crop or animal, often with the technical assistance available from Purdue University or the Purdue-supervised county extension service, or with specialized financing from a federal agency. The decline of the small farm brought on the development of the corporate farm.

Lemuel A. Pittenger was president of Ball State University from 1929 to 1942, presiding over the construction of a new library and assembly hall, fine arts building, women's and men's dormitory, and a expanded Burris Laboratory School. A Delaware County native, former rural teacher, and professor, Pittenger also served in the Indiana legislature after retiring from Ball State. Courtesy, Ball State University

The postwar population boom placed increased demands on Delaware County's public school system, which until the 1940s consisted of 12 separate school systems run by 12 township trustees, plus the Muncie and Albany system. As Muncie's schools experienced the most crowding, Muncie and Center Township school systems consolidated, removing the burden of educating the township's rural youth from the beleaguered township trustee and placing it on a new community school board. Several new elementary and junior high school buildings were erected, and other schools were enlarged. Muncie built its second high school, Southside, in the early 1960s, and the arrangement whereby Burris Laboratory School served as a city district school was terminated although Burris still operates as a state-supported school. The late 1960s saw the erection of a third city high school, Northside, followed in a few years by a new Central High School north of the business district. More recently the "baby boom" generation has completed high school, and toward the 1970s and 1980s Muncie's school system has faced the agonizing decision of closing schools because of decreased enrollment.

Changes in school districts wrought by population changes in the 1960s and 1970s also led to increased racial tension. A community segregated by residential districts, Muncie maintained a basically segregated school system in the elementary grades until the 1950s. Other institutions were segregated, too. Segregation was not, however, limited to schools. Blacks first gained admission to Tuhey Park's swimming pool in 1956 after city officials tried to provide a formerly private separate-but-equal swimming pool that later was closed. Segregation in movie houses and restaurants prevailed during World War II, and disappeared gradually. Although Muncie had black police officers for several decades, only in the 1940s were they assigned to patrol non-black neighborhoods as well, and only in the 1950s were blacks appointed to the city fire department, which by then had a force of more than 70 men. Utilization of school buildings in the 1950s and 1960s brought about bused integration and the melding of blacks into Southside High School, whose majority white constituency had proudly nicknamed its sports teams "The Rebels," was not without acrimony and conflict. Election of members of the black community to political offices, mostly minor but some major, helped ease the tension in the 1970s, although some tension still exists even as the community enters the final two decades of the 20th century.

In the rest of the county, consolidations in the late 1950s left only Monroe Township (Cowan), Salem Township (Daleville), and Mt. Pleasant Township (Yorktown) as single-township school systems. Washington and Harrison townships consolidated to form the Harrison-Washington school system; Liberty and Perry townships formed the Liberty-Perry system; and Delaware, Niles, Hamilton, and Union townships formed the Delaware Community system. All of the county schools boasted steady if not growing enrollment of high school students, plus stabilized or at worst not severely shrinking enrollments of children in lower grades.

With the exception of the school system in Hamilton Township (which took some "transfer" students from the part of Center Township that was not inside the Muncie corporation), Delaware County schools did not experience the crowding in the late 1940s and early 1950s that those in Muncie did. There was little building of schools before the 1960s, when state-imposed standards for elementary and secondary schools were updated.

The postwar education boom that the area was experiencing could not rival the growth of Ball State. What had been a teachers college with perhaps 1,000 students in the late 1930s had an enormous challenge in the mid-1940s when administration, faculty, and new president John R. Emens had to cope with hundreds of returning armed forces personnel who wanted to go back to school. College housing was even more scarce than city housing as enrollment tripled. Surplus war barracks and trailers were utilized in almost every available space within walking distance of the still-compact campus. Classrooms were full and faculty challenged to keep up with the new students, many of whom were more mature than students of pre-war days.

Ball State Teachers College built its first structure north of Riverside Avenue—the Practical Arts building—in 1950, starting a period of growth that would expand the campus more than 10 times over the next 30 years. In addition to building, the Emens administration also saw to the upgrading of numerous graduate departments and the establishment of the College of Architecture and Planning. The teachers college became Ball State University in 1965, three years before John Emens retired.

With the growth of the college and its place within the community came increased cooperation between Muncie and Ball State. A symphony orchestra began in 1949 as a joint college-community venture and quickly reached professional maturity. Plus the 3,600-seat John R. Emens College/Community Auditorium opened in 1964.

Muncie also continued to be a center for industry. Because of the demand for consumer goods, Muncie manufacturing establishments making glass products and automotive parts thrived in the years after World War II. In the early 1950s and again in the 1960s some factories returned briefly to manufacturing ordnance materials when the nation became involved in conflicts in Korea. However, changing national population patterns affected the economics of the glass industry, causing the termination of glass manufacturing in Muncie in the early 1960s. Ball Brothers shut down the last of its furnaces, keeping corporate headquarters and other operations in the city and locating newer factories closer to the markets for their products. Ball Corporation built a new international headquarters in downtown Muncie in the mid-1970s on the former site of Central High School.

John R. Emens, shown in an oil portrait by Bradford Lambert, was president of Ball State University from 1945 to 1968, presiding over its growth from a small teachers' college, through postwar years of increased enrollment and construction, to its development into a major university. University status was granted by the Indiana Legislature effective in 1965. Courtesy, The Muncie Star *and Ball State University*

Above: Ball State's Fine Arts building was completed in the late 1930s as a joint project of the Works Progress Administration, the college, and the Ball family. Ever since, commencement exercises were conducted each year on the building's south terrace. The size of the class indicates that this picture was taken sometime in the 1950s. Enrollment grew from about 3,000 immediately after World War II to more than 18,000 as the 1980s began. The college became a university in 1964. Courtesy, Ball Memorial Hospital

Top right: Ball State University conferred an honorary Doctor of Laws degree on George A. Ball in 1954. He had served on the Indiana State Teachers College Board (which operated Ball State) since the death of his next elder brother, Frank C. Ball. The youngest of the five Ball brothers, G.A. Ball died in 1955. Shown with him are John R. Emens, Ball State president from 1945 to 1968, and Richard Burkhardt, then dean of the faculty and the school's acting president in 1978-1979. Courtesy, Ball Memorial Hospital

Top left: Ball State Teachers College and contracting firm officials break ground for the L.A. Pittenger Student Center in 1951. Courtesy, Ball State University

Right: The Daniel Chester French statue Beneficence is shown on the Ball State campus in winter in this dramatic night shot. Photo by the author

"USE ONLY THE VERY BEST"
The WINNER SKATE.
Manufactured only by
A. L. JOHNSON & CO.,
MUNCIE, INDIANA.

Left: *A bronze casting of Cyrus E. Dallin's* Appeal to the Great Spirit *was installed as a memorial to Edmund Burke Ball along White River east of the Ball brothers' Minnetrista homes and near where the Munsee clan of the Delaware is believed to have had its village. Photo by Ruth Chin*

Far left: *A.L. Johnson & Company was only one of the five skateworks that manufactured roller skates in Muncie in the 1880s and 1890s. (Windsor)*

Top left: *In the early 1920s employees of the Indiana Steel and Wire Company could take part in a company band using instruments furnished by the company. The band posed on the steps of the Merchants National Bank in downtown Muncie. Courtesy, Floyd O. Kreider*

Above: *Wheeling Pike along White River northwest of Muncie was only a country lane when J. Ottis Adams rendered it nearly 100 years ago. Rising in the background of the scene is the clock tower of the third Delaware County Courthouse. The oil painting now hangs in the downtown branch of the Muncie Public Library. Courtesy, Muncie Public Library*

Above: A number of historic homes remain in Delaware County. Perry Township physician Samuel Vaughn Jump bought a farm near New Burlington in 1853 and began to build his residence there the same year. The house passed through several hands before it was placed on the National Register of Historic Places in 1983. Photo by Ruth Chin

Above right: Author Emily Kimbrough was born in this East Washington Street cottage in 1898 and lived there until she was 10. She wrote of her Muncie childhood in How Dear to My Heart, *published in the early 1940s. A number of her manuscripts are in the Stoeckel Delaware County Archives of Ball State University. The house was acquired by*

Historic Muncie, Inc., renovated, and placed on the National Register of Historic Places. The neighborhood has been designated the Emily Kimbrough Historic Neighborhood. Photo by Ruth Chin

Delaware County's third courthouse (left, 1878-1966) contrasts with its fourth (below). The County Building was constructed in the late 1960s, designed by the local architectural firm of Hamilton and Graham. The growth of government agencies has necessitated moving some agencies out of the building: a new structure is being planned to replace the nearby late-1950s county jail and augment the County Building. Photos by Ruth Chin

Opposite page, top: Charles Wesley Moore, who came to Muncie in 1830 from Portsmouth, Ohio, built this home at Washington and Mulberry (left) in 1844. His daughter, Mary Moore Youse, lived in the house as did her daughter, Mary Youse Maxon. Following Mrs. Maxon's death, the house was bequeathed to the Delaware County Historical Society. An interior view of the house (right) shows a piano believed to be the oldest in Delaware County. Photos by Ruth Chin

Right: Delaware County Fairgrounds hosted this horse show in 1960. Photo by the author

Left: Much of Delaware County has retained its ties to rural life and agriculture. Beef cattle are shown in a feedlot on the Keesling Farm near Muncie. Photo by J.C. Allen & Son, Inc., West Lafayette

Above: Large cornfields like this one north of Gaston are a common sight around the county. Photo by J.C. Allen & Son, Inc., West Lafayette

Following page: Historically, the presence of good sources of stone and gravel in Delaware County contributed to the area's early economic growth. Pictured is a modern stone quarry and gravel pit operation on County Road 350 North in eastern Delaware County. Photo by J.C. Allen & Son, Inc., West Lafayette

Above: Delaware County's Agricultural and Mechanical Society, sponsors of the Delaware County Fair, remodeled the fairgrounds' historic, 75-year-old grandstand in 1947. Less than a year later on a February afternoon, the grandstand burned to the ground as frustrated firemen watched: the fairgrounds, less than a mile from downtown Muncie, had no water mains or fire hydrants. Courtesy, James R. Bailey

Left: Locomotives of the Nickel Plate Road and its predecessor in Delaware County, the Lake Erie & Western, fueled up with coal at this station west of Muncie's business district until diesel locomotives replaced the steamers in the late 1950s. Courtesy, R.A. Greene

Changing manufacturing trends in the 1950s saw a former Muncie silverware company, Ontario Silverplate, dwindle and then grow, becoming a major international firm and manufacturer of forgings for the aircraft industry and related products under its new name, the Ontario Corporation. The Whiteley Malleable Foundry, an outgrowth of the Whiteley family's activities in the city that began with a shortlived venture to make reapers in the 1890s, became the Muncie Malleable Foundry before it was sold in the 1950s, shut down briefly, and reopened in the 1960s as Dayton-Walther Corporation. Nearby, the historic Kuhner Packing Company—in its final years the Marhoefer Packing Company—closed down in the 1970s, blaming its demise on changing patterns in wholesale meat distribution. The firm's closure meant the demise of Muncie's stockyards. Delaware County meatpacking thereafter was limited to the several custom butcher shops that had existed for many years.

Indiana Bridge Company, the firm that fabricated many of the steel bridges that revolutionized highway construction in Indiana and other mid-western states beginning in Gas Boom days, also diminished in importance as an employer in the 1960s but continued as a competitive force in the prefabrication of building steel. And although the Kitselman Brothers fence factory had shut down in the 1950s, the family's Indiana Steel and Wire Company became a major wire manufacturer, being acquired finally by General Cable Company. Numerous other steel and manufacturing firms continued to grow or die in Muncie. Warner Gear Company had merged with Borg and Beck into Borg Warner Corporation decades before, although it was still considered a Muncie and Indiana firm. A major manufacturer worldwide of automotive and marine transmissions, Warner Gear weathered the ups and downs of the automobile industry in the 1950s, 1960s, and 1970s, and in the mid-1980s was at high employment in its modern plant west of Muncie.

In addition to dominating several counties as a place for employment and retail trade, Muncie had become, in a quarter century, a major education center and was close to becoming a major regional medical referral center, both to the credit of those in the Ball family and others in the community who had decided to "go first class" with a new hospital and with the small private normal school at the west edge of Muncie.

Ball Memorial Hospital responded to the needs of the county's growing population by constructing subscription-funded additions in the mid-1950s and again in the mid-1960s, more than tripling the space for its patients. A decade later the hospital spent more than $25 million to replace part of its original late 1920s structure with a 10-story tower and to modernize completely its various departments. At Ball State University enrollments stabilized in the mid-1970s, shifting the school's emphasis from constructing residence halls to building additional classroom space for new disciplines.

Right: Dr. J. Sylvester Smith practiced medicine and surgery in Muncie at Ball Memorial Hospital in the 1940s and 1950s, later relocating in California. His departure left the community with no black physicians.

Far right: Postwar years brought a rise in Delaware County and the nation as a whole in civic involvement and voluntarism. This group of doctors' wives—one a doctor herself—met in 1949 to do some handiwork for the nurses' residence. The women were probably members of Ball Memorial Hospital Women's Auxilliary.

When Nellie G. Brown, a registered nurse, retired in 1952 after two decades as superintendent of Ball Memorial Hospital, doctors and community leaders on the hospital board honored her at a dinner. Miss Brown was succeeded by Walter G. Ebert, seated at the head of the table next to hospital board chairman G.A. Ball. Photos courtesy, Ball Memorial Hospital

Left: In the early part of the 20th century, Muncie cartoonist Chic Jackson achieved regional fame with this newspaper cartoon "Roger Bean." In the 1960s Anderson native Tom K. Ryan, raised and educated in Muncie, drew "Tumbleweeds" in his Muncie studio before moving to Florida in the 1980s. And in the late 1970s Fairmount native Jim Davis, a former Ryan assistant, created the cartoon cat "Garfield," which appears in more than 1,000 newspapers worldwide. Shown with his wife Carolyn and "Garfield," Davis opted to stay in Muncie and built a studio near the city. Courtesy, Ball State University

Far left: Author Emily Kimbrough wrote about her Muncie childhood in the early 1900s in How Dear to My Heart, *published in the 1940s. In 1981 she returned to her native city for ceremonies involving the restoration of the East Washington Street home where she was born and its placement on the National Register of Historic Places. She is pictured riding an old milk wagon in the Emily Kimbrough Historic District. Photo by Bruce Buchanan. Courtesy, The Muncie Star*

Below right: Members of the Muncie Police Department posed for a group picture on the steps of the Muncie Public Library around 1940. Courtesy, E.F. Petty

Outside Muncie little manufacturing was carried on for any length of time in Delaware County. Yorktown had a rockwool mill in the 1930s; Daleville had a firm that built schoolbus bodies. Eaton and Gaston enjoyed canning plants that had a wide market for their products, especially tomatoes and tomato products grown in east central Indiana fields. Eaton also had a paperboard mill and several smaller industries, and Albany had McCormick Brothers, manufacturers of specialty wire goods, until the 1970s. Also, because much farming was carried on in Delaware County, a number of towns and rural communities boasted grain elevators. The county's largest grain elevator in the latter part of the 20th century was operated by the Cross family at Oakville. Grain elevators—where grain was bought from farmers and shipped to larger centers for sorting and milling or resale—supplanted local milling firms in most Indiana communities by mid-century. Delaware County once again became a major wholesaler of food items with the growth of Marsh Supermarkets from a few small neighborhood stores in the 1930s and 1940s to a large chain of supermarkets; its main office and warehouses at Yorktown made Marsh Supermarkets the community's major employer for more than a quarter century beginning in the early 1950s.

In addition to jobs, improved schools and services—like fire and police protection—brought new residents to Delaware County's unincorporated areas. This growth in population proved an incentive for residential building outside Muncie and the county's incorporated towns.

As the nation neared its Bicentennial, sociologists continued—using the vast amount of data already compiled about the area—to study "typical America." According to reports that came out in the 1970s, if Muncie and Delaware County were typical of America, then America was not in bad shape at all. Muncie and Delaware County had survived their first 150 years quite well, and were looking toward the future.

CHAPTER VII

Partners in Progress

Photographed in 1936, Home Cafe on West Seymour Street was a popular spot in the south portion of Muncie's business district. Courtesy, Floyd O. Kreider

Artists and artisans have left their marks on Delaware County. The county may be viewed as a reasonably flat, rectangular canvas, originally daubed with various shades of green rising from the thick, black soil. Pioneer families added tiny pointillist dots to this painting; these dots blended into communities. By the 1850s many areas that had been haphazardly green in summer took on the orderly appearance of having been planted by man. The greens turned to gold. Planners and developers added straight lines to the landscape: town squares, roads, and fence rows.

In the late 19th century a new pigment—the orange glow of natural gas wells—seemed to erupt from the surface of our canvas. New smokestacks appeared and, beneath a haze, there developed a focal point which this picture had previously lacked. Muncie, the Magic City, grew from what had been Muncietown. It became an economic center as well as the political county seat.

Yet, as the rivers of Delaware County run fast in the spring and slow to a trickle during late summer droughts, the orange bursts weakened and eventually retreated from the scene. No matter; by 1900 the scene had been changed irrevocably. A sense of partnership had developed among the business leaders of this community, and the self-styled Magic City would discover its real magic in the resilience, resourcefulness, and determination of its people. Brush strokes on the canvas of Delaware County have been scrutinized repeatedly by a parade of social scientists following the "Middletown" studies of the late 1920s. These dilettantes have admired the pervasive influence of the Ball family and others, while concluding with remarkable agreement that the work is truly that of no single partner.

Muncie emerged in the 20th century as a regional center for education and health services, while continuing to nurture its industrial economic base. The area's progress is not attributable to any accident of nature, location, or politics, as much as to the spirit of such entrepreneurs as are featured on the following pages.

MUNCIE-DELAWARE COUNTY CHAMBER OF COMMERCE

Every Tuesday evening in 1894, and for several years thereafter, the Commercial Club of Muncie held a meeting. Sometimes there was no quorum, but members met anyhow, to enjoy a "smoker" or a lecture, or just to talk about new opportunities for business expansion in the Magic City.

What kept men coming to these meetings may have been a sense of history unfolding so fast as to require weekly reviews just to stay informed. But the members did more than meet. They raised money to provide factory sites and start-up capital for businesses relocating in Muncie. They offered "bonuses" based on employment. And they traveled to investigate the soundness of some firms who seemed perhaps too anxious to receive an offer of cash and a plant site.

During one meeting in 1904 the club members watched with interest as a chimney sweep device was demonstrated. Then they considered an inquiry from a hoop factory and referred it to the committee on manu-

facturing. The same committee would later recommend approval of a plan to assist a boiler factory (Broderick & Quinlan), report favorably on the proposed expansion of the Ontario Silver Works, and consider plans of an unidentified steel wheel factory and a brass foundry.

The club sought valiantly to aid in the continuing operation and sale of the American Roller Mill, and to find ways to help the neighboring Normal City Commercial Club in its effort to assure continuance of the Indiana State Normal School, now Ball State University.

The Commercial Club of Muncie constructed its own building in 1918 on ground purchased in 1902 from James and Margaret Boyce. Hardly had the club name been carved in the handsome limestone facade of the building on the northwest corner of Main and Jefferson streets when the name of the group was changed, and the Chamber of Commerce was born.

Gradual changes included

The Muncie-Delaware County Chamber of Commerce is located at 500 North Walnut Street.

employment of a full-time professional staff. A new office facility was constructed to house the Chamber on North Walnut Street in 1957. Weekly membership meetings gave way to multiple meetings involving a 15-member elected board of directors and 16 committees. The program of work includes operation of a Small Business Assistance Center and the Muncie Area Growth and Industrial Council (MAGIC).

A "Muncie's Future Seminar" was conducted in 1983 to begin a long-range planning effort which encompasses many areas of interest to local residents. Although the basic focus of the Commercial Club has remained constant in the Chamber, the scope of the latter organization extends more broadly to preservation and improvement of the quality of life in general for Muncie and Delaware County.

ELM RIDGE CEMETERY

By 1926 Muncie had clearly surpassed its gas boom era and entered a period of more orderly, but still dynamic, growth. Convinced that continued expansion would cause the existing municipal cemetery to run out of space, the founders of Elm Ridge Cemetery started to develop 20 acres of an 80-acre tract between Kilgore Avenue and the White River west of

Situated amid the serene landscaping of the cemetery grounds is this bronze replica of a Giovanni Strazza statue.

The mausoleum at Elm Ridge Cemetery is one of the largest in the Midwest and noted for its design, bas-relief carvings, and exquisite choice of marble.

Muncie. The new cemetery officially opened the following year.

Founders were D.O. Skillen, Charles E. Watkins, Effie W. Skillen, James E. Watkins, Sr., and Will F. White. In later years the cemetery became wholly owned by members of the Watkins family. James Sr. was general manager until 1972, when he was succeeded by his son, James Jr. Father and son have each served as president of both state and national cemetery associations.

Elm Ridge has developed very few lots larger than 12 spaces. Its emphasis on two-space "companion" lots was unique in 1927, when larger family plots were customary. A focal point of the cemetery is its mausoleum, which was begun in 1930 with 888 crypts. This nationally renowned structure has grown to 4,500 spaces, making it exceptionally large for a city of Muncie's size, and ranking it among the largest mausoleums in the Midwest. The building is noted for its design, its bas-relief carvings, choice of marbles, quality of construction, and furnishings.

By late 1983 Elm Ridge Cemetery had expanded to own more than 105 acres, slightly more than half of which have been developed. More than 13,000 interments have taken place there. The cemetery employed 15 persons in 1983, including Arthur Ballinger, Jr., vice-president of sales, who has been associated with the cemetery since 1936.

Elm Ridge Cemetery was the first in its area to provide a music system of chimes, and was a pioneer in the development of garden-type sections, where landscaping and hedges provide background for smaller monuments. During World War II, when real estate development was suspended, cemeteries could not add sections. Lots were subdivided. The use of smaller lots became more common, and the garden-type section concept evolved when cemetery expansion was resumed in 1946.

There are areas for lawn-level and traditional above-ground memorials, the mausoleum, and indoor and outdoor niches for cremated remains. Two chapels are available for committals or full funeral services at Elm Ridge Cemetery.

WARNER GEAR

The Warner Gear Division of Borg-Warner Corporation, during the '50s, achieved an employment peak of 5,000—making it Muncie's largest employer. Two decades later it appeared to be fighting for survival—a fight it seems to have won.

Resilience, determination, and entrepreneurship are characteristics that repeatedly dot this firm's history and the attributes of character are not those of a single person, but of several. And the history of Warner Gear is inextricably bound into the history of Muncie and the city's business sector.

The story and the 20th century began together. Tom, Henry, and Hugh Warner were operating a small shop making telephone equipment they had invented and perfected. The invention used magnetic coils to make telephones ring.

Long on ideas but short on capital, they involved the owner of another Muncie firm, Glascock Brothers Manufacturing Company, in their second industrial venture. Abbott Livingston Johnson had already acquired the Glascock firm, and under his direction it became involved in a variety of products. But Tom Warner was a partner with Abbott Johnson in the enterprise that became Warner Gear.

Johnson and Warner started making auto accessories in a small, dirt-floored barn at 928 East Charles Street, using a gasoline engine as a power plant. In 1901 the firm had eight employees— about all the building would hold with room for equipment.

Ray Johnson, son of Abbott, is credited with demonstrating a "differential" at a 1903 New York automobile show where Ransom E. Olds gave him an order for 4,000 units. Abbott L. Johnson II, grandson of the co-founder, recalls that Hugh Warner

was the one working on a "sliding-gear transmission" which he, Ray Johnson, and the senior A.L. Johnson sold to the Hudson Motor Company on a visit to Detroit. Hudson bought 1,000 units, according to Johnson. The company pioneers then borrowed money from the Delaware County National Bank to buy the machinery and start building transmissions.

Warner Gear was off and running. It has never stopped. The telephone equipment venture became Warner Electric Company, later Warner Machine Products. It was sold in 1970 to Essex International, since merged with United Technologies. Glascock Brothers Manufacturing has also expired. But the "spin-off" of these

firms has continued to grow and prosper.

Tom Warner left the company that bears his family name in 1910. He was apparently persuaded by Will Durant, who was then forming General Motors, to go with him to Toledo to start a transmission plant there. Warner reportedly sold his stock in Warner Gear to the Ball brothers of Muncie, who were already involved in another industrial success story of their own. Ironically, Warner was sued by his former partner, A.L. Johnson, and subsequently left General Motors in a disagreement with Durant. He

The Warner Gear plant, 1918 to 1977.

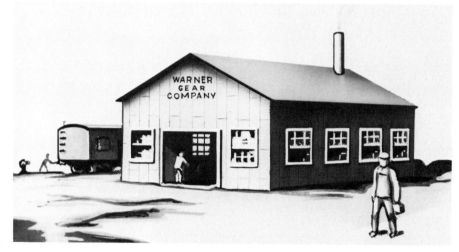

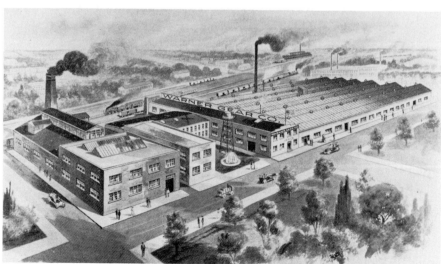

An artist's rendering of the original Warner Gear Company building, circa 1901.

moved to California, according to A.L. Johnson II.

The company purchased a whole city block for major expansion in 1918. A second major new product, a standardized three-speed manual transmission, was introduced in 1926. In 1928 the company became part of a four-way merger to create Borg-Warner Corporation, a $39-million corporation. Borg & Beck, Marvel Carburetor, and Mechanics Machine Company were the other parties to this merger, creating a new giant among automotive suppliers. Charles Davis of Warner Gear, son-in-law of A.L. Johnson, who had died in 1923, became Borg-Warner's first board chairman.

In 1930 the division built the first part of what is today its headquarters and manufacturing plant at the west edge of Muncie. Several additions and changes preceded the consolidation of Warner Gear activities at this location, and the concurrent closing of its Seymour Avenue facilities in 1977. The older structures and grounds were donated to the City of Muncie as part of an economic development plan endorsed by the city administration.

The Depression reduced orders for Warner Gear products but in 1932 a new product, the self-contained overdrive unit, was introduced. Within two years it became the third major product for this division, which discontinued its original product, the differential, in 1927. Significantly, Warner Gear has altered its product line several times to stay abreast of market opportunities. In 1950 the division's automatic transmission became a fourth major product. Yet the company was no longer making the automatic transmission when a fifth major product line, four- and five-speed manual transmissions, came to the forefront of production in 1981.

Resilience and determination are characteristics nurtured at Warner Gear. Its continuance and growth may be expected to result from the same innovative spirit that permeates its past and present.

Charles S. Davis of Warner Gear, with J.R. Francis and George W. Borg (left to right), met in 1928 to form Borg-Warner Corporation.

The present home of Warner Gear extends along Kilgore Avenue at the western edge of Muncie. The facility contains more than 1.5 million square feet of manufacturing and office space.

BALL MEMORIAL HOSPITAL

Ball Memorial Hospital is now a 674-bed regional referral center serving the health care needs of people throughout eastern Indiana.

More than a half-million patients have been admitted and cared for at Ball Memorial Hospital since it opened its doors on August 8, 1929. And hundreds of thousands more have been treated on an outpatient basis.

For Ball Memorial Hospital those decades have represented years of growth and caring. Ball Hospital has grown from a community hospital of 142 beds and 18 bassinets to a regional medical referral and teaching center with 674 beds and 55 bassinets. It has grown from 2,302 patient admissions its first year to 21,330 patient admissions in 1983. Today Ball Hospital, one of Muncie's largest employers, is one of the five largest hospitals in Indiana and is among the top five percent of hospitals in the United States in terms of size and the wide range of special diagnostic and treatment services offered.

In the early 1920s the Home Hospital at 1128 South Mulberry Street served Muncie citizens with accommodations for 80 patients—but it was obvious community needs were outgrowing the Home Hospital's capacity. One Muncie citizen who was

genuinely concerned about the need for establishing an adequate hospital was Edmund B. Ball, one of the five Ball brothers from Buffalo, New York, who had established the Ball Brothers Corporation in Muncie.

Edmund Ball served as a trustee on the Home Hospital board and when overcrowding became a problem he offered an alternative to enlarging the existing facility. He said if the state legislature would pass a bill authorizing Delaware County to build and maintain a new hospital, he would see that the necessary funds were provided for the entire project. The bill passed, and Ball State Teachers College provided the grounds for the new hospital. This act initiated a strong bond between the two institutions that has been evident in nursing education, medical schooling, and community health education programs over the years.

The Ball Memorial Hospital Association was formed in 1925 and it initiated the plans for a new hospital and a residence for nurses with the Ball family pledging assumption of the necessary expenditures. Although Edmund Ball died while these plans were still in their preliminary stages, his bequest of $3.5 million helped start the Ball Brothers Foundation which

underwrote all of the hospital's early construction.

While Muncie citizens expressed gratitude for the new facility, many felt its capacity was far in excess of the foreseeable needs of the community and surrounding area. But they were soon proved wrong, and the physical facilities of the hospital have been growing to meet community and area needs ever since.

The hospital's laundry building was completed in the fall of 1929, and in January 1930 Maria Bingham Hall (named after the mother of the five Ball brothers) opened with housing accommodations and teaching facilities for 104 student nurses. These two structures and the main building housing patient rooms and ancillary services represented a $1,722,095 gift to the Muncie community—the first major gift of the Ball Brothers Foundation.

Patient admission more than doubled in each of the hospital's first two decades of service, and the Ball Brothers Foundation continued to help

Jack Reichart, a Muncie inventor and manufacturer, is shown with the "homemade" iron lung he constructed to help meet the needs of Muncie's polio epidemic.

the hospital meet the increasing demands on its services.

Thanks to the foundation's generosity, Ball Hospital survived the Depression years when it was often hard to make enough money to keep operating. And the foundation also provided funds for the Edmund Burke Ball Medical Building which opened in 1937, increasing the hospital capacity to 224 beds.

But the 1940s brought their own problems. The war years saw an extreme shortage of physicians and nurses, and 1949 saw Muncie in the throes of a severe polio epidemic with 120 reported cases in Delaware County. The way in which Ball Hospital and the Muncie community joined hands to handle that epidemic made news all across the country as local manufacturers supplied the hospital with iron lungs made from steel alcohol drums and vacuum cleaners while nurses, doctors, and volunteers worked around the clock. The response to this crisis seemed to herald what has since become an increasing awareness of the importance of combining the resources and skills of Ball Memorial Hospital and the community to meet community needs.

The Isabel Urban Ball Rehabilitation Center, another gift of the Ball Brothers Foundation, was opened in 1951. During the years immediately following, an increased patient population and rising construction costs indicated that a large amount of funds would be needed for future Ball Hospital expansions. In 1953 a community hospital campaign organization invited the public to contribute to a $1.7-million construction fund. The Muncie

Groundbreaking ceremonies for Ball Memorial Hospital took place on June 7, 1927.

community responded generously, and when the goal was exceeded by one million dollars the building committee asked for an additional $975,000 to meet the area's growing health care needs. People again demonstrated their appreciation of Ball Memorial Hospital by pledging $1,235,000. With the addition of $168,000 in federal funds, these contributions built the seven-floor wing on the west side of the hospital which opened in July 1957. The hospital now had a total of 450 beds.

By 1963 it was necessary to stage another fund-raising campaign with a goal of $2.5 million. A total of $2,755,000 was pledged and federal funds of $1.5 million were received to erect the five-story 196-bed east wing. A total of $1.3 million in funded

depreciation also went toward the east wing construction.

The 10-story tower, which opened in June 1979, was financed by $13,865,000 from funded depreciation and limited term rates, and $8,720,000 in loans. This addition includes 320 beds—many of which were replacement beds for ones previously located in the hospital's older buildings. With the new tower came the addition of more than $1.5 million in new X-ray diagnostic equipment as well as the expansion of such areas as the intensive care unit, the coronary care unit, laboratory, obstetrics, surgery, and the emergency suite.

This early 1930s aerial of Ball Memorial (looking northwest) shows the original complex of buildings— the main hospital structure with its north and south wings, the laundry facility directly to the south, and Maria Bingham Hall, a residence and training center for nurses, to the southeast of the main building.

Following the tower's opening, a $3-million remodeling project of the hospital's other buildings enabled it to greatly expand many of its other services. In fact, the expansion of Ball Hospital services has been an obvious priority during the '70s and '80s. Services added in the past decade include open-heart surgery, acute and renal dialysis, an oncology unit for cancer patients, C-T scans, total joint replacement surgery, ultrasound procedures, nuclear medicine, an out-patient cardiac rehabilitation program, a hospice program for terminally ill patients, and a chemical dependency unit for alcohol and drug abusers.

Despite its emphasis on expanded facilities and services and its continuing commitment to educating and training tomorrow's medical practitioners and technicians, Ball Hospital has consistently managed to keep its costs from 15 to 25 percent below regional and national averages for hospitals its size.

Six people have been responsible for overseeing much of the hospital's growth and planning over the years. Nellie Brown was superintendent of the hospital from 1932 to 1952; Walter Ebert was administrator from 1952 to 1972; and Roy Erickson has served as president of the hospital since 1972. Ball Hospital's three board chairmen have been Frank C. Ball, who was elected at the hospital's first formal board meeting in 1928 and served until 1943; George A. Ball, who served from 1943 until 1955; and Edmund F. Ball, who has served as chairman since 1955 and has served on the board since 1932. Also helping to establish the hospital's basic policies and long-range goals, as well as general guidance to meet those goals, have been the 51 dedicated Muncie citizens who have served on the hospital's board of directors over the years.

It is the people of Muncie—from the community philanthropists, benefactors, and activists, to the

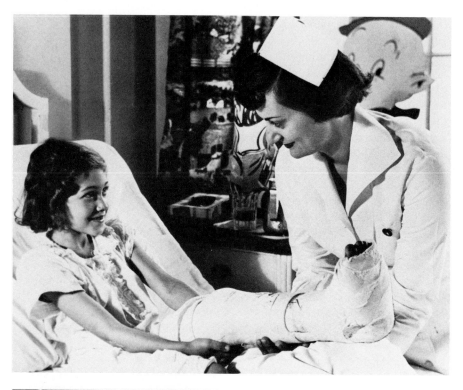

Elizabeth Burke, R.N., takes care of pediatric patient Joyce Griffith in this 1952 photo.

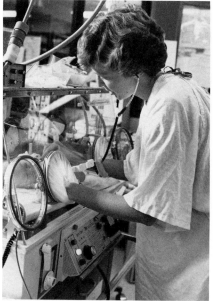

This 1983 photo shows neonatologist Donna Wilkins, M.D., examining baby Laura Elaine Stern in Ball Hospital's special care nursery.

dedicated hospital employees to the caring volunteers—who have made Ball Memorial Hospital the major institution it is today. These statistics reflect what was happening at Ball Hospital on a single given day by mid-1983: 512 inpatients were at the hospital; 59 new patients were admitted; 6 babies were delivered; 411 outpatients were treated; 41 operations were performed; 372 X-rays were performed; 87 emergency room cases were handled; 1,828 laboratory tests and examinations were conducted; 1,466 patient meals were served; and 9,193 pounds of laundry were processed. On that same typical day, $95,514 was paid in salaries to hospital employees and $21,023 was spent on supplies.

There's something else that goes on at Ball Hospital every day, too: planning. Ball Hospital is studying the health care needs of eastern Indiana residents and how it can best meet those needs today and tomorrow. Why? Because Ball Hospital is committed to making its second half-century of growing and caring as dynamic as its first.

A.E. BOYCE CO., INC.

Four lines of business—office furniture, office supplies, printing, and bookbinding—are housed in a Muncie commercial building which won a national award in 1966 for store design. The building houses A.E. Boyce Co., Inc., which has more recently extended its property east along the north side of Jackson Street for a full block, from Jefferson to Elm. In a separate building is Boyce's design center, started in 1980, offering showrooms and turnkey interior design services. Perhaps expectably, one of the design center's first accomplishments was an extensive interior redesign of Boyce's own award-winning retail establishment.

"We're good at finding answers for people's problems in environment,

The modern home of A.E. Boyce Co., Inc., won a Geyer Award for store design in 1966 and replaced the facility which had been "home" for 61 years.

flow of materials, communications, etc.," explains company president David A. Galliher. "We practice what we preach in our own operation."

Galliher's grandfather, Arthur Earl Boyce, founded this business in 1899. He was succeeded by David's father, Robert J. Galliher, who became chairman of the board when his son

became president in 1967. The venture started as a bookbinding shop, located on the second floor of the Boyce Block at Main and Jefferson streets. (The building was named for the founder's father, James Boyce, one of Muncie's pioneer leaders.) The firm moved to the corner of Main and Elm streets a year later, and added a printing department.

In 1904 the Hoosier Printing Company (as it was known until 1912) occupied a narrow building at 321 East Main, and this was the company's home for 61 years. During that time, Galliher recalls, it was necessary for all forms and paper used in printing operations to be transported between floors by a hand-pulled elevator at least two times in each direction. The building was dirty, had no hot water, and was air conditioned only in the accounting office. Retail items were often reached by ladder.

Despite these inefficiencies A.E. Boyce Co. grew. The founder copyrighted accounting systems for various types of business. Ring binders and post binders made in Muncie were sold nationally. When the Indiana State Board of Accounts required that all government agencies use state-prescribed forms for all record keeping, A.E. Boyce Co. became, and remains, the largest supplier of these forms in Indiana.

In 1978 the firm purchased the Didier Printing Company in Ft. Wayne, which operates as a wholly owned subsidiary.

A.E. Boyce (left) and salesman William C. Woods try out a Maxwell automobile, circa 1910, in front of the firm's building at 321 East Main Street.

DELAWARE COUNTY ABSTRACT COMPANY

During the 1880s it was not uncommon for attorneys in many American cities to begin a specialization in abstract work. Gradually this specialty evolved into separate abstract and title companies.

It may be argued that the abstract business was uncommonly brisk in Muncie, where the Industrial Revolution began with a boom from newly discovered natural gas wells. The industrialization of the nation's economy clearly meant that many new urban centers would be established and grow with related commercial and residential development activity. This era of urban growth would gradually transform the country as large farms would give way to smaller parcels of individually owned property, and property transactions would increase in number.

Muncie's gas boom accelerated this transition and the revolution refused to stop when the gas wells faltered. Indeed, according to John V. Meredith, president of Delaware County Abstract Company, this area's period of industrial expansion "really continued until the Great Depression."

John V. Meredith ought to know. The firm he now heads was formed by his grandfather, John F. Meredith, and the grandfather's brother, Elmer, in 1887. As a third-generation attorney and abstractor, John V. Meredith now operates one of Muncie's oldest firms with continuous family ownership.

The concern was incorporated in 1901 as Delaware County Abstract, Title & Loan Company. It represented several lenders as correspondents. However, some time after the death of the founder in 1931, the words "Title & Loan" were dropped from the firm's name.

The first office faced the courthouse from the southwest corner of Main and Walnut streets. When that three-story facility was razed to erect the six-story Wysor Building, the abstract business moved around the corner to 110 North Walnut.

The Depression had a marked effect on the company's history, almost ending it. Joseph T. Meredith succeeded his father just as this time of trial was beginning. The demand for abstract work dwindled. Finally down to one employee, an office assistant, Joseph Meredith cut his own salary to pay her. He also went into politics, and was elected to serve one two-year term as county treasurer.

Joseph Meredith died in 1953. John V. Meredith joined the firm in 1949 after earning his own law degree. In 1962 the Delaware County Abstract Company moved to 117 North Mulberry Street, its present home.

BEN ZEIGLER COMPANY, INC.

Ben Zeigler, who founded the company that bears his name, in 1917.

Sherman Zeigler, son of the founder, is president of Ben Zeigler Company, Inc.

Ben Zeigler grew up near the German border in Russian-dominated Lithuania, from which he emigrated to Indiana as a young man in the early 1900s. His uncle, Joseph, had started a metal scrap business in Anderson, and Ben went there to be outfitted by his uncle with a horse and wagon. "The horse was mostly dead, the harness mostly wire, and the wagon mostly junk," he later recalled. He then went to southern Indiana and toured farm areas, buying obsolete farm equipment for resale as scrap.

The German farmers in southern Indiana could basically understand Ben Zeigler's Yiddish, giving him more time to learn English and to become acquainted with the ways of his adopted country. But this way of life was unpredictable at best, and when the young man married he reasoned that he might improve on his business fortunes by relocating from Osgood,

Indiana, to Muncie, which even then enjoyed the reputation of being a highly industrialized city. Ben Zeigler would concentrate exclusively on industrial scrap.

The year was 1917. His one employee earned 20 cents an hour. Ben was in business near the railroad lines at Seymour and Mulberry streets.

The enterprise prospered. By 1920 it was ready to move to a location with its own railroad siding. It found one at 801 South Council Street.

Ben's son Sherman joined the Navy during World War II. Sherman's former classmate and neighbor, William K. Rogers, joined the Army. When both came home in 1946, the business was ready to receive its second generation of leadership. The Ben Zeigler Company incorporated with Sherman as president, Ben as vice-president, and Rogers as secretary/treasurer. (Rogers retired in 1973.)

The venture moved to a new location in 1948 and expanded into scrap iron and steel brokerage. An office, warehouse, and new rail

facilities were built expressly for Zeigler at 500 West 23rd Street. From this location, nonferrous, ferrous, and alloy scrap are now processed and shipped to steel mills and foundries throughout the United States, although Zeigler's primary business area is within a 300-mile radius of Muncie. Despite rail availability, 80 percent of the firm's shipments in the 1980s are by truck. Throughout its expansion Zeigler has maintained its founder's original concept in handling only industrial plant scrap.

When Ben Zeigler died in 1976 he was widely mourned. Muncie and the nation had lost a good citizen. Ben's son continues a tradition of civic involvement, and—through the Ball State University Foundation—a Ben and Bessie Zeigler Fund brings world-renowned speakers to annually address a campus and community audience. It is a fitting memorial.

BALL CORPORATION

This company, one of the nation's largest, operates manufacturing facilities in 15 states and two foreign countries. In 1983 it reported total sales in excess of $909 million.

Although the world's only "fruit jar museum" occupies a conspicuous area in Ball Corporation's world headquarters, the company's leading product in 1982 sales was the metal beverage can. More glass containers were sold to commercial food marketers than were produced for home canning purposes, and yet Ball jars and lids continue to be a most visible segment of this diversified enterprise.

Packaging—in glass and metal—accounted for 71.1 percent of Ball Corporation's 1983 sales. The remainder was divided between industrial and technical product groups. Industrial products include coextruded plastic sheet and containers, injection-molded plastics, metal decorating, and rolled zinc. A Ball plant in Tennessee is the country's principal source of copper-plated zinc blanks from which pennies are coined by the U.S. Mint. The technical products group includes aerospace, electronic systems, and agricultural systems divisions—all representing technologies on the leading edge of the 1980s industrial frontier.

John W. Fisher, chairman of the board, has called Ball a "packaging company with a high-technology base." Sales have more than doubled since the firm first sold its stock to the public in 1972, but the spirit of expansion is well rooted in this enterprise, which was founded in Buffalo, New York, in 1880.

Five sons encouraged by their mother to work together gave their name to the Ball Brothers Glass Manufacturing Company, which located in Muncie in 1888 and produced glass here until 1962. Although the business retained some operations at Buffalo and Bath, New York, for a short time after the start-up in Indiana, Muncie was unquestionably to be the firm's headquarters.

Credit for attracting this industrial giant-to-be into Delaware County is largely given to James Boyce, an enthusiastic member of the Muncie Board of Trade, which preceded the Muncie Commercial Club and Chamber of Commerce.

Frank C. Ball had been visiting in Ohio, considering possible industrial sites at Findlay, Fostoria, and Bowling Green, when a communication from Boyce piqued his curiosity and led him to visit Muncie. He would later recall in his memoirs that he was not very impressed by the city itself but that "the men were all courteous, kind, and businesslike." A contribution of $5,000 from a citizen's fund to help relocate a factory site of seven acres and promises of a gas well and a private rail connection cemented the agreement.

The Ball brothers came to Muncie

The Industrial Revolution came to glass blowing with this semiautomatic glass-forming machine for wide-mouth containers, patented in 1898 by F.C. Ball.

William C. Ball, Frank C. Ball, Edmund B. Ball, George A. Ball, and Lucius L. Ball (seated) 1893

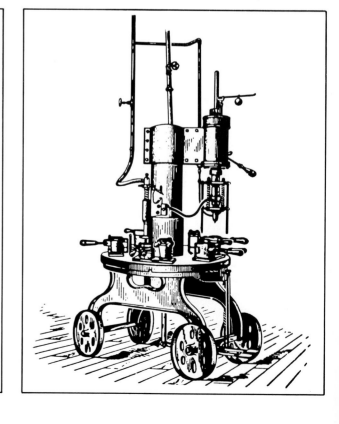

Although Ball Corporation now maintains manufacturing facilities in 15 states and two foreign countries, its headquarters remains on High Street in Muncie.

and built adjacent homes on the north bank of White River. Mrs. George Ball, having been informed by Buffalo friends that she would be moving to Indian territory, excitedly told her husband that she had seen "the fires of Indian encampments" as her train moved west into Muncie at night. Her husband laughed and told her that what she had seen were the flambeaux of natural gas wells. No matter; the romanticism of being in a community which had not long ago been a true Indian settlement led to the naming of Minnetrista Boulevard in front of the Ball homes. The name came from "minne," an Indian word for water, and "tryst," meaning an agreed meeting place. The George Ball residence is now used as a guest home for corporate visitors.

When plant obsolescence and economic realities mandated the closing of a glass plant, paper box plant, rubber plant, and zinc mill—all located in Muncie—some local critics felt that the company was abandoning its adopted hometown. The retention of research facilities, corporate offices, and the enlargement of these notwithstanding, the announcement in the 1970s that a new four-story office building would be erected in downtown Muncie was viewed by some with relief. Ball Corporation clearly did not intend to leave nor to diminish the importance of this community in its corporate expansion.

The site chosen was that of the former Muncie Central High School, which was replaced by a modern structure north of the business district (on the grounds of what was once the Minnetrista Golf Course, across the river from the Ball residences).

The total of civic and charitable contributions made by the Ball

brothers, their families, and the company they founded will never be known. The university, hospital, YMCA, YWCA, Masonic temple, and American Legion buildings owe their existence in whole or part to Ball largesse. It is also reported that Muncie's financial institutions survived the Depression as the Ball brothers unilaterally guaranteed all deposits.

A total of 11,306 persons—mostly Muncie residents—contributed $31,965 to help erect a statue honoring the Balls' beneficence, in 1937. The last work of sculptor Daniel C. French was placed on the Ball State campus. The dedication address included these words:

All this is a tribute alike to the city of Muncie and to the Ball family. The Balls have acted more as the social trustees than as the personal owners of the fruits of their competence. And Muncie has had the rare good sense to know good citizens when it sees them.

MARSH SUPERMARKETS, INC.

Customer self-service was an innovation of this first Marsh store, opened in Muncie in 1931.

Prior to the 1930s it was common for Muncie residents to walk into a neighborhood grocery store and ask the friendly storekeeper or an assistant for the items wanted. The store employee found each item in stock and returned it to the open counter beside the cash register.

Ermal Marsh changed all that. In 1931 he opened the first store in what would become one of the Midwest's largest food retail organizations. He introduced to Muncie a new concept in grocery retailing, allowing customers to serve themselves by finding merchandise on shelves or display racks.

Marsh was a Ball State University student when the enterprise that would become Marsh Supermarkets, Inc., was born. He was well prepared to carry out his ideas, both by education and by family background. His father, Wilmer Marsh, had set the stage for such a venture when he purchased the Morehous Brothers grocery in North Salem, Indiana, back in 1922.

Ermal Marsh's company offices were in an old house behind the first store on West Jackson Street. By 1983 that building was still standing, but virtually everything else about the firm had changed. Corporate offices were relocated along with a main warehouse covering 10 acres in the southwest quadrant of Yorktown. A refrigerated warehouse for perishable goods, built in 1981 immediately west of the main warehouse and office complex, includes 125,000 square feet of floor space. All areas of the new warehouse are equipped to provide precise temperature and humidity controls, and produce is arranged to permit rapid computerized order processing.

By 1947 Ermal Marsh's company required a fleet of five trucks to serve the Marsh Foodliner system, as the chain was then known. In 1983 the truck fleet comprised 44 tractor units and 135 trailers, operating from a total of four warehouses to serve 76 Marsh supermarkets. The average supermarket occupied close to 26,000 square feet and had 1982 sales of $6.7 million.

In addition to the supermarkets, Marsh operates 140 Village Pantry convenience stores served by a separate distribution center. The first Village Pantry was opened in Muncie in 1966. The balance of 222 retail outlets in Indiana and Ohio includes five "Farmer's Market" produce stores (one in Muncie) and one "Foxfires" restaurant (also Muncie based). Of the supermarkets, nine are classed as

Wilmer Marsh bought this store in 1922 at North Salem near the Indiana-Ohio line. Wilmer's son, Ermal, founded Marsh Supermarkets in 1931.

"Marsh X-tra" stores and combined with pharmacies. Specialty departments in Marsh stores offer floral items from a Marsh-owned greenhouse, film-processing services from a Marsh-owned photo lab, and delicatessen items supplied from a Marsh-owned commissary.

The innovation that characterized Marsh operations from the beginning has continued. The company was a pioneer in unit pricing and open-code dating. Marsh led the world in the use of electronic scanning at its check-out lines in Troy, Ohio. Marsh is also believed to be the first to have installed energy-management systems in its stores. These systems not only sense and control the energy consumption of all store equipment, but provide instant warnings of equipment malfunctions through computer monitoring of the system at central headquarters. This unique concept has resulted in considerable savings to the firm in utility expenses in addition to

Typical of "Marsh X-tra" stores, including pharmacy, flower shop, bank, deli, and bakery, is this one in Muncie at 3910 West Bethel Avenue.

Don E. Marsh, president of Marsh Supermarkets, Inc., since 1968.

Ermal Marsh, founder, in 1957. Ruth Chin, photographer.

philosophy would be continued as his brother, Estel V. Marsh, took over. In 1968 Estel Marsh became chairman of the board and Ermal's son, Don Ermal Marsh, was named president.

Don Marsh succeeded his father and uncle after 15 years of preparation,

All company personnel are encouraged to take active roles in their communities. The firm contributes each year to many philanthropic programs and supports youth organizations with donated merchandise, special discounts, and the use of

providing more efficient equipment maintenance, thereby preventing merchandise deterioration.

Ermal Marsh voiced this philosophy: "The solidarity of our progress and growth is in direct proportion to the kind of service we give to our customers." His untimely death in 1959 shocked the food industry in which he had become a highly respected leader. His business

during which he held various positions starting as a part-time store employee and advancing into various executive posts through duties as an assistant store manager, dairy and frozen foods buyer, personnel trainer, and public relations director. A graduate of Michigan State University, he has been active in numerous professional, political, community, and fraternal organizations.

Marsh stores and parking lots, in addition to monetary contributions. Marsh also underwrites many cultural, religious, and entertainment programs such as the National Sports Festival in Indianapolis and the Conner Prairie Symphony Series. But the greatest contribution in this area is probably that of personal time and involvement on the part of many of Marsh's more than 7,000 employees.

BRODERICK CO., DIVISION OF HARSCO CORPORATION

Von E. Rains, president of the Broderick Co., is a native of Montpelier, Indiana. This Blackford County community 25 miles north of Muncie also gave birth to the Broderick Co. more than a century ago. But there is no family connection; the similar origins are merely coincidence.

More than a coincidence is the fact that a village blacksmith shop may be regarded with historical accuracy as the forerunner of modern metal-forging operations. This industry, which uses the slogan "Forging a Stronger America," began in just such a way, in the town of Montpelier in 1882. By the turn of the century it had become Broderick & Quinlan, manufacturer of steam boilers.

Caught up in the natural gas boom of the era, the firm grew rapidly and moved to Muncie in 1905 with support from the Commercial Club. Also known as M.H. Broderick & Sons Boiler Works, the firm located at 500 Lincoln Street on the south side of the "Big Four" railroad. Several additions and modernizations have taken place since, but the press-forging activities of this local industry continue at the same Muncie site. The company discontinued boiler production during the early part of World War II.

In 1935 the firm acquired a drop hammer-forging plant north of the railroad which had been started in 1910 by the Dean Brothers from Massachusetts. This facility, with auto access from East Jackson Street, is now known as the Broderick Hammer Plant, using air-powered hammers with up to 6,000-pound force to shape metal products for various industrial customers.

Joseph Broderick sold the 74-year-old family-owned company in 1956 to the Harsco Corporation, an inter-national corporation headquartered in Harrisburg, Pennsylvania, with operations in four major product fields: primary metals, construction, fabricated metals, and defense. Broderick is one of 16 divisions in the Harsco Corporation.

Early in 1970 Harsco installed forging presses in a plant owned by

This pre-1980 photo shows the Muncie operations of the Broderick Co. The hammer plant is located to the left of the railroad; the press plant and offices are on the right.

the corporation at Kenton, Ohio, and this plant was added to the Broderick Co. as part of the division entity. The three plants accounted for $73 million in sales in 1979. Products are hammer, press, and upset forgings ranging from three to 100 pounds, custom-made to rigid specifications for customers such as Caterpillar, Rockwell International, Dana, Mack, Eaton, John Deere, J.I. Case, Borg-Warner, Muncie Chevrolet, and some 70 other manufacturers mainly in farm, heavy truck, and off-highway equipment products.

The Broderick plant, with offices in the building at left, appeared this way in the early 1900s.

WESTINGHOUSE ELECTRIC CORPORATION

George Westinghouse (1846-1914) revolutionized American society by perfecting the transformer, which makes possible the transmission of electricity at high voltages over long distances and the local distribution of power at lower voltages.

These huge 1,200-kilovolt generator step-up transformers were built at Westinghouse's Muncie plant.

Westinghouse Electric Corporation has been recognized as a leader in the power transformer industry ever since company founder George Westinghouse pioneered development of the first commercial transformer back in 1886.

Today that tradition of excellence continues at the Muncie plant complex of the firm's power equipment division. The Muncie facility was built in 1961 exclusively for the design, development, and manufacture of the world's largest power transformers. Such equipment is required by electric utilities in order to carry electricity efficiently over long distances from a generating plant to the ultimate user.

The Muncie plant has been credited over the years with numerous industry "firsts," including the design and manufacture of some of the world's largest transformers in terms of their power capacity and overall size. Other products manufactured at Muncie include furnace transformers for industrial applications and various specialty transformers such as phase

angle regulators.

An ongoing product improvement program at the Muncie plant is aimed at maintaining the company's technological leadership in the electric utility industry. The primary mission is to develop power transformers that in the future will be smaller, more energy efficient, and less costly to produce.

Coupled with this extensive redesign effort has been a multimillion-dollar plant investment

program, begun several years ago to provide the facility with the tooling and equipment necessary to become the low-cost producer of highly reliable products.

Complementing the plant's product improvement and facilities modernization activities has been a continuing effort to improve product quality and productivity. For example, through such grassroots efforts as quality circles and value engineering teams, employees at all levels of the organization are becoming actively involved in solving work-related problems and improving the way they perform their jobs.

Westinghouse believes in being a good corporate citizen in the communities in which it maintains plants and offices, and Muncie is no exception. The company encourages its employees to become engaged in

Shown here is an aerial view of the Westinghouse plant in Muncie. The 700,000-square-foot facility was built especially for the manufacture of power transformers for the electric utility industry.

local civic, cultural, and other community organizations.

As one of the Muncie area's largest industrial employers, Westinghouse generates a major economic impact upon the local community in terms of payrolls, taxes, and local purchases.

INDIANA VOCATIONAL TECHNICAL COLLEGE— REGION SIX

Region Six of Indiana Vocational Technical College (Ivy Tech) serves a seven-county district of east-central Indiana from Muncie. Ivy Tech divides Indiana into 13 regions to provide career training programs and occupational skills updating. Courses offered are divided into four major divisions: trade and technical, business science, health occupations, and graphics and media. Students may enroll for individual courses or work toward an occupational or technical certificate or a two-year associate of applied science degree.

Ivy Tech was a creation of the Indiana state legislature in 1963. The regional board was chartered in 1968, but the school did not flourish in this area until 1970-1971, since which time it has grown significantly.

Because Indiana has had no community college system for post-high school education, offering only traditional academic four-year programs (with the exception of Vincennes University, a two-year institution) the concept of Ivy Tech filled a unique need in the state for higher-level public education.

Region Six students may choose from courses in computer programming, numerical control (CAM), drafting and design (CAD), word processing, integrated circuit design, engine control systems, automotive, information processing, accounting, professional development, industrial-business management, secretarial, building construction, health care, and certification occupations.

Richard L. Davidson, regional vice-president/dean since 1980, coordinates activities in three Muncie buildings as well as branch operations in Marion, Anderson, Elwood, and New Castle. The Muncie "campus" is comprised of two leased buildings and one owned

by Ivy Tech, all located on a tract of some 15 acres in the Muncie Industrial Centre industrial park complex.

The quarters are vastly different from those near downtown on South Council Street, where the regional operations began in 1968, or a Liberty Street location which served as the school's second site. Area banks were "very supportive" of Ivy Tech's need to grow, Davidson notes, with almost every county in the region represented in the financing of the school-owned headquarters building. The facility project was approved in 1976 at $1.7 million over a 12-year period.

Region Six conducted its first classes in 1968 for relatively few students. Fall enrollment in 1983 was 2,266.

In addition to providing a structured educational program, Ivy Tech offers a system for efficient employee training and skills upgrading, working with business and industry to meet specific manpower training needs on a custom basis, in plant or college facilities.

One of Ivy Tech's facilities is located on a 15-acre tract in the Muncie Industrial Centre.

MERCHANTS NATIONAL BANK OF MUNCIE

Delaware County's largest financial institution is the Merchants National Bank of Muncie, which surpassed $300 million in assets in 1982. The bank is the largest in east-central Indiana and ranks 17th in the state on the basis of year-end 1982 financial reports.

Organized on February 3, 1893, the bank was located at the northeast corner of Main and Mulberry. In 1904 it moved to a new building at the northwest corner of the same intersection. A major decision to move from leased quarters to a "home of its own" resulted in acquisition of land and construction of a magnificent classical-revival building of Indiana limestone at the northeast corner of Jackson and Mulberry streets. Muncie architect Cuno Kibele designed the new facility, which opened on July 6, 1914. The total construction cost was just under $45,000.

This building housed Merchants National until 1972, when it was replaced by the present five-story structure on the same site. The new building was erected largely to the north of the old one, and the transition was gradual as the south facade of the new $3.5-million headquarters was completed only after the 1914 structure was torn down.

Bank officials discussed starting branch activities as early as 1947 and acquired property for the South Madison branch the following year. This branch was not completed until June 18, 1951.

Merchants National's first drive-up banking facility was established at the Madison Street branch early in 1958. Its popularity led to additional drive-up banking facilities.

Data-processing equipment was first used in 1962 and the first electronic computer was installed three years later. The Indiana Steel & Wire office building on East Jackson Street was acquired in 1967. The Data Center was opened at this location on August 7, 1972.

The original bank, at Jackson and Mulberry streets, was razed to make room for this five-story structure, completed in 1972. Today there are 300 employees at this and 13 other locations.

Installation of MoneyMover 24-hour tellers during the summer of 1981 provided a new service for customers: the convenience of 24-hour banking.

When Merchants National opened for business in 1893 it had three employees. At the close of the second day of business, deposits totaled $9,560 and loans amounting to $2,550 had been granted. The bank's capital was $67,470. Checking accounts and short-term loans were the primary services. All entries were made manually with pen and ink. Passbook savings accounts were not accepted by Merchants National until 1914.

Today the bank has almost 300 employees, with capital in excess of $25 million and assets exceeding $320 million. Electronic data processing of records has added to operating

Designed by Muncie architect Cuno Kibele and constructed of Indiana limestone, this was the first "real" home (1914-1972) of Merchants National Bank.

efficiency. With 13 locations and 6 MoneyMover 24-hour tellers, Merchants National offers a full range of financial products to meet the needs of its customers.

MUNCIE STAR AND MUNCIE EVENING PRESS

Two separate and distinctive newspapers have shared facilities in Muncie since 1947, the year following their consolidation under one ownership. In 1981 the three-story building which had been the home of Muncie Newspapers, Inc., was enlarged to extend from Jackson to Main along the west side of High Street. The *Muncie Star* and *Muncie Evening Press* editorial staffs each had new homes but were still separate entities. To encourage journalistic quality a spirit of competition has been nurtured, particularly between the news staffs of these publications.

The two newspapers reached 86.4 percent of Delaware County homes in 1983—ranking first among Indiana newspapers for metropolitan area coverage, and among the top newspapers in the nation in terms of this circulation measurement.

Historically, the Muncie newspapers' consolidation climaxed a trend toward mergers beginning early in the 20th century, ending an era of personal journalism which saw many communities smaller than Muncie

More than 50 years after first being named sports editor, award-winning Muncie Star *retiree Bob Barnet still writes a weekly editorial column.*

Looking southwest from Main to Jackson Street, the 1981 editorial offices addition adjoins the older three-story structure which has been given a completely new facade.

boasting rival publications.

The *Muncie Star,* founded by George F. McCulloch, began its existence in 1899 at 107 West Main Street. In 1905 the *Muncie Evening Press* was born as a consolidation of the *Muncie Herald* and the *Muncie Times,* and was located on North High Street across from the courthouse. The *Press* had several owners prior to 1910, when George B. Lockwood bought the newspaper and moved to Muncie from Marion.

The *Star's* ownership changed two times: in 1904 when it was sold to John C. Shaffer, and in 1944 when Eugene C. Pulliam acquired it. Two years later Pulliam also bought the *Press* from George Lockwood's heirs.

Pulliam, founder of the national journalistic society Sigma Delta Chi at DePauw University, became the owner of a group of newspapers. Still operating independently with associated ownership are newspapers in Indianapolis, Muncie, Vincennes, and Phoenix, Arizona. Eugene S. Pulliam is publisher and executive vice-president, and William A. Dyer, Jr., is president of Muncie Newspapers,

Although a tape-driven Linotype accelerated production over keyboard operation, the hot metal typesetting methods were abandoned by Muncie Newspapers in 1974, replaced by "cold type" which is photographically reproduced.

Inc. Robert G. Ellis is vice-president and general manager; Frank E. Russell is secretary/treasurer; Wiley W. Spurgeon, Jr., is executive editor.

Through the years many employees of both the *Star* and the *Press* have achieved outstanding records in career service. The *Muncie Press* moved in 1918 to High and Jackson streets, where the papers combined almost 30 years later. The *Press* was edited by Wilbur Sutton throughout these events and until his death in 1949. Willard C. Worcester moved from circulation manager to general advertising manager of the *Press* and became general manager of both newspapers after consolidation, until his retirement in 1972.

The *Star* historically has been the larger of the two newspapers in circulation, carrying more state and national news, while the *Press* circulates mainly in Delaware County and its editorial emphasis reflects this. *Star* editorial columnist Richard A. Greene has become a resource for

historic information about east-central Indiana, and indeed has witnessed much of it himself. Robert L. Barnet, sports editor of the *Star* for more than 50 years, somewhat reluctantly retired from a career which had earned him Indiana Basketball's Silver Medallion and a position as one of only four newsmen to be inducted into the Indiana Football Hall of Fame.

Several employees of the Muncie newspapers can claim 40 to 50 years of service, and those with only a decade or two are apt to be regarded as newcomers.

The conversion to "cold type" in 1974 ended an era of Linotype composition and metal stereotype preparation by the newspapers' production departments. It resulted in a gradual decline of employment in the department, from 70 to about 40, accomplished through attrition. In all departments, the two newspapers in 1983 employed 180 full time and 60 part time, plus some 450 carriers (who work as independent contractors) and 35 motor route and truck drivers.

The first issue of the *Muncie Press* in 1905 was an eight-page newspaper which represented the maximum capacity of its flatbed press. The *Star* had installed a new press in 1900, which had to be moved in 1905 when the "new" *Star* building at the southeast corner of Mulberry and Adams streets was occupied. The relocation aroused national attention as a large force of expert mechanics was required to dismantle the press and move it piece by piece to be reconstructed in the new location without missing an issue.

Less trauma may have accompanied the newspaper's 1981 expansion on its half-block site in downtown Muncie, but there has been no less amount of pride in this new 75,000-square-foot facility which is the present home of Muncie's two daily newspapers.

Pouring "pigs" is a function that disappeared from Muncie Newspapers during the 1970s. The "pigs" were suspended above and gradually melted into a heated pot on a Linotype, where the lead alloy was molded into lines of metal type.

MAXON CORPORATION

Several Muncie-based companies trace their origins to the late 19th-century gas boom, but one Muncie industry was founded as a direct result of that era's demise and the replacement of private wells with natural gas piped into Indiana from West Virginia and other states. This company, Maxon Corporation, manufactures industrial gas and oil burner equipment and valves. Its products are used by many different types of industry throughout the world.

The Maxon Corporation story starts in 1910, when a group of Chicago financiers formed the Dawes Holding Company to acquire and consolidate small gas utilities. This group bought the two principal gas companies then serving the Muncie area and hired John H. Maxon, manager of the local gas utility in Gallipolis, Ohio, to come to Muncie and merge the two properties.

Two younger brothers of John H. Maxon—H.R. Maxon and J. "Jack" Maxon—had been involved in construction work including the building of pipelines from West Virginia gas and oil wells to surrounding industrial areas. It was logical that they soon joined their

J. Jack Maxon (left), Harry R. Maxon, Sr. (center), and John H. Maxon (right) founded the Maxon Corporation in 1916.

brother to work for newly formed Central Indiana Gas Company on a large gas storage holder, a main gas pipeline to Marion, Indiana, and related construction projects.

Industrial plants seemed a likely market for the new utility, but it soon became apparent that the conversion from local gas to pipeline gas was not a simple matter. The crude burners that had been used locally were wastefully inefficient. Further, the more sophisticated heat processes involved oil burners using compressed air or high-pressure steam for atomization, because gas burners could not supply high enough temperatures.

At the old Dean forge plant it was pointed out that raw gas flames simply blew away from the pipe nipples without supplying the required heat concentration. John Maxon felt that his brother H.R. would be just the one to solve that problem, enabling his gas company to replace the oil burners and thus acquire a major new customer.

H.R. Maxon accepted the challenge and developed a burner combining the

principle of a Buffalo Forge blower used in blacksmith shops with that of the chemical laboratory burner previously developed in Germany by R.W. Bunsen. Connecting a gas pipe to the air inlet of the blower meant that fuel and air were thoroughly mixed before being introduced into the furnace that heated the steel for forging.

This became the Maxon Premix Burner. Brother Jack produced the necessary parts in the gas company's machine shop. One by one, adaptations of this burner allowed other industries to convert to gas, and the Dawes group noticed the gas sales results. They encouraged H.R. Maxon to secure patents on his combustion devices, and they helped finance a new company to manufacture these units and market them nationwide.

This was 1916. The next year a small building, formerly a piano factory, was acquired along the belt railroad on Muncie's south side between Jefferson and Mulberry streets, where a small crew, headed by Jack Maxon, began the manufacturing operations. In later years there would be many additions to this property and, in the 1960s, the original factory itself would be

H.R. "Red" Maxon, Jr., is shown testing a Maxon shut-off valve. Photo circa 1947.

replaced by additions to more recently constructed facilities. By 1983 the Maxon Corporation occupied some 200,000 square feet of industrial and office space on four blocks adjoining its headquarters on the southeast corner of 18th and Mulberry streets.

The company's history was not one of consistent growth and expansion, however. The Depression years, problems with patent infringement, and competition abetted by defection from within took serious tolls on Maxon Corporation's fortunes. There was, however, a continuing emphasis on product improvement and adaptation which resulted in the firm's survival and recovery from each setback to new and greater achievement.

The Premix Burner was followed in time by a Wide-Range Burner™ which H.R.'s son, H.R. "Red" Maxon, invented. To this were later added the AIRFLO® Burner and the OVENPAK® Burner. These products were refined several times and adapted to meet the special needs of different industries— to dry grain, to bake food, to melt metals, even to destroy air pollutants by "after-burning" industrial plant emissions.

"Red" Maxon became president of the organization during the 1960s. Other members of the management team in this decade of growth were Harrold Hays, Charles Rothhaar, Lowell Crouse, and Bob Yeo. During those years employment doubled, sales volume tripled, and substantial acquisitions and plant expansions were made.

Maxon International was formed in 1966 in Belgium, where a

manufacturing facility was added in 1972. The Okadee Controls Company, a sole supplier of shut-off valve bodies to Maxon, was also acquired in 1966 with operations moved from Michigan to Muncie.

By 1983 U.S. employment by Maxon Corporation stood at 234, compared to a peak of 275 reached in 1982.

Company officers in 1983 included Charles Rothhaar, chairman of the board; Robert Smitson, president; William Pingry, Bruce Brenneman, Jack Brunette, and Charles Hetrick, vice-presidents; Reed Cheesman, treasurer; Don Mitchell, controller; Bob Beavers, secretary; and Bill Coppin, assistant vice-president.

The firm now occupies 200,000 square feet of industrial and office space on the four blocks adjoining the headquarters building at 18th and Mulberry streets.

ONTARIO CORPORATION

Ontario Corporation's beginnings date to 1882, when the Ontario Silver Company was formed in Welland County, Ontario, Canada, to manufacture silverware. The firm was acquired in its early years by Leonard L. McGlashan of Welland County, and Gardner C. Clarke, a physician from Niagara Falls, New York.

As their enterprise prospered, the two men decided to enter the U.S. market. High tariffs on Canadian-made products led them to build a U.S. plant. In early 1895 McGlashan and Clarke came to Muncie, a boom town after discovery of natural gas, and committed to building in the Magic City on land provided free by the Citizens Enterprise Company, a forerunner of the Chamber of Commerce.

By late summer in 1896 Ontario Silver was producing silverware in a new plant west of White River and north of West Jackson Street. Over the years ownership passed from McGlashan and Clarke to Clarke's heirs, to Leo S. Ganter, Sr., and in 1944 to National Silver Company, New York City. National Silver operated the plant until 1955, when it ended six decades of silverware-making in Muncie.

National's pullout led to creation of the modern-day Ontario Corporation. William W. Rich, a former executive of Oneida and R. Wallace & Sons, both silverware-making firms, came to Muncie in 1953 to run the old Ontario for National Silver. He bought the plant and some old forging equipment. In early 1956 the new Ontario began producing close-tolerance forgings, mostly of stainless steel and largely for the aircraft industry.

The new Ontario aggressively pursued acquisition of heavy equipment needed to forge aircraft engine components. As the size of engines increased, ever-larger forge presses were required to shape metal into almost any configuration by exerting thousands of tons of pressure on a red-hot "billet."

Under Rich, Ontario also embarked on what became a continuous program to improve the appearance of its plant and to substantially reduce exterior noise from forging presses and other equipment. This good-neighbor attitude still guides the company.

Early stress on quality workmanship—critical to aircraft engine reliability—paid quick dividends. By 1960, after only four years in business, Ontario was approved as a supplier of titanium fan blade forgings for jet engines. Employment levels marched steadily upward, moving hand in

Although Ontario Corporation's operations have become international in scope, its headquarters remains in Muncie on West Jackson Street.

Leonard L. McGlashan, in partnership with Gardner C. Clarke, founded the Ontario Corporation. The firm was moved to Muncie in 1895.

William W. "Bill" Rich was president of the firm from 1955 until his death in 1963.

Van P. Smith has been president of the corporation since 1963.

hand with increasing sales.

Unexpectedly, Rich died in 1963. His stepson, Van P. Smith, succeeded Rich as Ontario's chief executive and has continued in that role for two decades.

The '60s brought rapid growth. Three additions and a new office facility were built at the West Jackson Street plant. Ontario acquisitions included the John M. Sherry Laboratories in Muncie; and Pyromet, Inc., a technologically sophisticated heat treating and brazing company in San Carlos, California. Ontario principals also created an industrial park, adjacent to the Delaware County Airport, which later became an Ontario subsidiary.

Growth continued in the '70s and '80s. Superior Metal Treating Corporation, a subsidiary created in 1957 and first housed in Ontario's Jackson Street plant, changed its name to Pyromet Industries and moved to Ontario's industrial park. Ontario also acquired a machining operation, CDS

Engineering, San Jose, California; a forging plant at Pontypool, South Wales, United Kingdom; and Dulond Tool & Engineering, Sarasota, Florida, an aerospace-related machine shop doing custom work for the U.S. military. The corporation also owns a controlling interest in Oil Equipment Services Inc., Houston, Texas.

A building at 13th and Madison streets has become the new home of Sherry Laboratories. The former Industrial Trust & Savings Bank building in downtown Muncie was purchased and remodeled to serve as corporate headquarters.

Although international in scope, Ontario's heart still beats in Muncie. For more than a quarter-century, Ontario has stressed involvement in community, state, and national affairs. Ontario people are active in a variety of civic organizations, and serve on local governmental bodies, state regulatory agencies, and other public commissions.

Smith, a former legislator and past chairman (and still member) of the Indiana Commission for Higher Education, sets the example by involving himself in nearly all significant community activities. In 1983 he assumed the role of vice-chairman of the Chamber of Commerce of the United States and is chairman for 1984-1985.

Ontario today is one of the world's largest forgers of airfoil components and one of the largest independent forge shops in the world. Its unique combination of forging and metal-lurgical skills allows the company to work any alloy into any size or shape for aerospace customers. It is a major supplier of "after-market" engine component repair services to commercial airlines throughout the world and to the U.S. military. Ontario is pursuing a future in forging non-engine aircraft components and beginning to diversify into other non-aircraft fields.

MUTUAL HOME FEDERAL SAVINGS AND LOAN ASSOCIATION

Readers of the *Muncie Daily Times* found this announcement in their paper shortly after a Saturday night meeting on September 7, 1889:

Secure a Home.
The books of the Mutual Home & Savings Association are now open. Every person interested in saving money or securing a home should become members at once.
Office, Room 4, The Anthony. Chas. E. Jones, President. Geo. N. Higman, Sec.

Mutual Home's modern office building on the northwest corner of Charles and Mulberry streets.

In fact, George N. Higman had come to Muncie five years before to enter the real estate business and had opened a loan department to encourage home buyers. The horizon was, according to a previous county history, "aglow with the flames of thousands of gas lights" when Higman persuaded Charles Jones and others to meet with him in his office in the Anthony Block on Walnut Street for the purpose of organizing a new building and loan association.

One of those present was George W. Ewing, who sought a $400 loan from the association. Receipts totaled only $230 that evening, so Ewing was persuaded to accept a $200 loan instead. As collateral he pledged his home at 1115 West 10th Street. The loan was to be repaid at a rate of no less than 50 cents a week, of which no more than 24 cents could be applied to interest. Ewing later became a well-known contractor in Delaware County. His loan was fully repaid on February 22, 1901.

George Higman continued to serve as the association's managing officer until the 1920s. Under the terms of the original organization, the managing officer was not a director, and the president's duties did not traditionally extend into day-by-day management. Elected to the board of directors in 1921, and to the office of president two years later, Higman transformed that office into a more active one. Until his death in 1940, at age 83, the founder was so identified with this institution that it was sometimes referred to as "the Higman loan."

In the early 1900s Mutual Home was located on the northeast corner of Charles and Mulberry streets.

George N. Higman founded Mutual Home & Savings Association in 1889.

The corner of Charles and Mulberry streets became the site of Mutual Home's first association-owned office building in 1906. Two other offices were rented after the firm outgrew the second-floor office in the Anthony Block (which was on the northwest

An early rented office of the firm at 109 East Adams Street in Muncie.

corner of Jackson and Walnut streets). Located on the northeast corner at Charles and Mulberry, Mutual Home's office was enlarged by additions during the next 57 years.

When the First Presbyterian Church relocated from the northwest corner of Charles and Mulberry to Riverside Avenue in 1955, Mutual Home acquired the old church property and eventually converted it to a parking lot. In 1963 a new Mutual Home building was opened to the public on the former church site, and the parking lot was eventually relocated with an auto drive-up facility where the former office building had stood.

George Higman was succeeded as managing officer by James Clawson in 1921, Walter C. Burt in 1964, and Gene B. Kern in 1971. The title of president was accorded to the managing officer during Burt's administration. Also at that time the association changed from being a state-chartered association to a federally chartered one. Reviewing the association's history, Kern noted, "we have not been struck so much by the changes over the years as we have by the consistencies." Each managing officer advanced to that position after years of service and retired to continue

serving on the board of directors.

The growth of Mutual Home has been greatest in recent years. While it took Mutual Home 82 years to reach its first $100 million in assets, it took only six more years to double that figure. During this same period of dynamic growth, staff size increased from about 50 to more than 100. In 1968 Mutual Home opened the first branch office of a savings and loan association in Delaware County.

Mutual Home "convenience centers" are now found at four Muncie locations, and in Yorktown, Winchester, Warsaw, and North Webster.

The Winchester Home and Savings Association of Randolph County was also merged into Mutual Home in 1975. The Warsaw and North Webster facilities were established through merger in 1981.

Mutual Home joined the "Money-Mover" 24-hour teller system, the state's largest network of automatic teller machines, in 1983. At the same time Mutual Home agreed to become part of the "Plus System" national network of teller machines, to provide maximum convenience for its traveling customers wishing to obtain cash from checking accounts in other cities. One of the Mutual Home "MoneyMover" machines was located inside the Muncie Mall for the convenience of shoppers there.

The association continues to explore new opportunities in financial service and expects to begin its second century of operation with the same enthusiasm, courage, and business acumen that has characterized its past and present.

The interior lobby of Mutual Home's facility at Charles and Mulberry in the mid-1950s.

113

BALL STATE UNIVERSITY

When the five Ball brothers of Muncie donated the campus and buildings of the defunct Muncie National Institute to the State of Indiana in 1918, Ball State University was founded. At first the institution was the Eastern Division of the Indiana State Normal School; in 1922, in recognition of the beneficence of the Ball brothers, the board of trustees gave the school the additional name of Ball Teachers College. In 1929 the college became independent of Indiana State and was renamed Ball State Teachers College. Thus it was to remain until 1965, when, acknowledging the college's growth, the state legislature designated the school Ball State University.

In addition to Muncie National Institute, several other short-lived

The original campus structure, with many renovations, has been preserved as the Administration Building at Ball State.

One of the more recent additions to the campus is the Alexander M. Bracken Library, named for a past president of the board of trustees who also served as chairman of the board of the Ball Corporation.

predecessors had occupied the campus. Eastern Indiana Normal University opened in 1899, only to close in 1901. The campus was next home to Palmer University (1902-1904), followed by Indiana Normal School and College of Applied Science (1905-1907) and Muncie Normal Institute (1912-1917); the name was changed to Muncie National Institute in 1913.

As the college developed into a

university, it was inspired and guided by the men who have served as its presidents. These leaders are William Wood Parsons, also president of Indiana State Normal School, 1918-1921; Linnaeus Neal Hines, 1921-1924; Benjamin Jackson Burris, 1924-1927; Lemuel Arthur Pittenger, 1927-1942; Winfred Ethestal Wagoner, acting president, 1943-1945; John Richard Emens, 1945-1968; John J Pruis, 1968-1978; Richard W. Burkhardt, acting president, 1978-1979; Jerry M. Anderson, 1979-1981; and Robert P. Bell, 1981-1984.

Ball State has grown to the point where it serves about 18,000 students

from more than 40 states and 60 foreign countries. The university comprises six colleges: the College of Applied Sciences and Technology, the College of Architecture and Planning, the College of Business, the College of Fine Arts, the College of Sciences and Humanities, and the Teachers College. The colleges offer a total of 125 undergraduate, 85 master's-level, 18 doctoral-level, and 14 specialist-in-education programs. The university confers about 4,400 degrees each year.

In the spring of 1932 master's-degree programs were instituted; the first master's degree was granted in 1934. In 1947 a sixth-year program was initiated, and in 1948 Ball State and Indiana University inaugurated a cooperative doctor of education degree in several fields of education. A similar cooperative agreement leading to the doctor of philosophy degree was developed with Purdue University in 1957 in the field of guidance and counseling. A program leading to the specialist in education degree was

Familiarly known as "Benny," this statue entitled Beneficence *was placed on campus by Muncie residents to memorialize the philanthropy of the Ball family.*

offered for the first time in 1959. Doctoral programs leading to the doctor of philosophy and doctor of education degrees were instituted in 1961 and the doctor of arts degree in 1971. In October 1973 the National Council for the Accreditation of Teacher Education granted Ball State full accreditation for all graduate programs through the doctorate in fields of education. In March 1974 the North Central Association of Colleges and Secondary Schools granted Ball State final accreditation at the doctoral level.

The General Assembly of the State of Indiana created the statewide medical education system in March 1971 and established Centers for Medical Education in cooperation with existing medical and educational institutions, including Ball State.

The years have seen a number of special facilities established on the 955-acre campus. They include the Center for Energy Research, Education, and Service; a planetarium and observatory; the Alexander M. Bracken Library, with more than a million books, periodicals, and micro-forms; the Institute of Gerontology, which offers the only state-approved graduate program in gerontology in Indiana; Computing Services, with a broad range of software for use on mainframe, mini-, and micro-computers; and the Human Performance Laboratory, one of the finest research facilities in the world for the study of human bioenergetics and physical stress. There is one outdoor laboratory on campus—Christy Woods, a beautiful patch of Indiana forest—and three others are nearby—Ginn's Woods, Sixteen Acres, and the Esther L. Cooper and Robert H. Cooper Memorial Woodlands.

As a member of the Mid-American Conference, Ball State participates in 18 intercollegiate sports—nine for men and nine for women—including football, basketball, field hockey, swimming, and volleyball. For its Artist and Concert series, the university annually brings to the modern 3,600-seat Emens Auditorium well-known professional performers in plays, musicals, and symphonies. And throughout the year Ball State offers film series, special workshops, and seminars. Among these are annual summer workshops for high school students in journalism, theater and interpretation, and computer science and applied mathematics, as well as the Mid-America Music Clinics. Another popular summer offering is Elderhostel, a program of inexpensive week-long classes for senior citizens; courses include history, physical fitness, and contemporary Chinese culture.

As Ball State looks to the future it will continue to produce outstanding leaders, public servants, and public figures.

The "greenhouse" addition to the College of Architecture and Planning serves as a solar-heating laboratory for the Center for Energy Research, Education, and Service.

THE MEEKS MORTUARY

Robert Meeks (left) and Isaac Meeks (right), co-founders of The Meeks Mortuary. Recognized as the oldest firm in Muncie, it began in 1844 as R. & I. Meeks — specialists in furniture manufacturing. The undertaking part of the business was added later.

The name of the village was still Munseytown when Robert and Isaac Meeks came to Delaware County from West Virginia with their parents, Amos and Nancy Means Meeks. The brothers worked as apprentices for pioneer furniture makers John Nottingham and Job Swain from 1841 to 1844, when they bought out their employers and continued the business as R. & I. Meeks on the northwest corner of Main and Jefferson streets. (After fire destroyed the furniture shop the land was sold to James Boyce, who constructed the "Boyce Block," best known in the 1980s as the home of the Muncie Civic Theater and adjacent retail shops.)

Within a few years the firm had added undertaking to its furniture business, and by 1866 it was already recognized as the oldest firm in Muncie. "Indian Jim," the last of Delaware County's original settlers, died within the next decade and records since discovered in the basement of the old county courthouse disclose that the Meeks firm was paid $10 for his funeral.

Furniture and funeral businesses were commonly associated in those times, and the Meeks firm apparently excelled in both. Several area homes still prize Meeks-built furniture items fashioned from walnut, cherry, oak, and ash. When the company moved to the southeast corner of Elm and Washington, and later to a two-story sales building at 115 East Main Street, it was truly a family enterprise with three of Robert's four sons — Martin, James, and Will — involved.

Isaac and Robert died in 1891 and 1906, respectively. James and Will Meeks retired, but the family tradition continued as Martin's sons, Arthur and Ernest, joined their father in acquiring the business, which then became M.L. Meeks and Sons. The furniture line was discontinued, and soon a younger son, Charles, also joined the firm.

M.L. Meeks died in 1928, and in 1932 his sons erected the present structure at 415 East Washington Street in his memory. One of the first facilities in the nation designed and built specifically as a mortuary, it also includes a crematory.

The present organization is headed by David Martin Meeks, son of Arthur and a great-grandson of co-founder Robert Meeks. The Meeks Mortuary has a large professional staff committed to continuing its longtime policy of providing quality service at an affordable price. It is a point of pride with this firm that in nearly 140 years no family has ever been denied a Meeks service because of its financial situation.

MUNCIE AVIATION CORPORATION

The name "Muncie Aviation" is applied to one of the largest and oldest Piper aircraft dealers in the nation, the largest aircraft sales and service dealer in Indiana, a nationally recognized avionics supplier, engine, parts, and accessories dealer, and to the firm that manages Johnson Field, the Delaware County Airport.

The retail assets of Muncie Aviation Corporation were sold in 1974 to the Minnetrista Corporation, and the name "Aircraft Distributors of Muncie" was adopted for that portion of the business whose total activities are represented by sales to a dealer organization handling new and used airplanes. Aircraft Distributors of Muncie now represents Piper throughout Indiana and Ohio. Muncie Cheyenne Sales, also a division of Minnetrista Corporation, sells turbo-prop aircraft in an area comprising Michigan, Indiana, Ohio, Kentucky, and Tennessee.

The two companies employed 87 persons by late 1983. The payroll includes a service department with 19 mechanics and one of the Midwest's largest avionics departments, employing eight technicians.

By whatever name, the service and sales facilities housed at the Delaware County Airport have become widely known in general aviation circles, and private flying has made the field one of the area's busiest. (The only commercial flight service at Muncie in 1983 was provided by Britt Airways, Inc., with commuter flights to South

Bend and Chicago.) Muncie Aviation was incorporated on March 14, 1932, as a dealer for Waco aircraft. Within a year sales and service for Beechcraft and Aeronca were added. In 1936 the company became one of the original Piper distributors, using the Piper J-2 Cub, one of Piper's first models, as its demonstrator.

The airport originally started with one half-mile-square grass landing area, outlined by perimeter lighting using Ball fruit jars as reflectors. The first paved runway was built in 1945.

Muncie Aviation maintains 60 Piper Cheyennes for corporate customers in Indiana and surrounding states. As Piper's first factory-certified repair station, Muncie Aviation also services all of Piper's piston-engine line. Mooney Aircraft has just been added as a new product line.

The private airport was deeded over to the county in 1956, when federal funds became available to expand the field into a functional municipal airport.

In addition to the main hangar constructed in 1932, additional hangars have been provided to house some 85 Muncie-based aircraft. Muncie Aviation's sales and administration building, constructed in the 1960s, ranks as one of the finest physical plants of its kind in the Midwest.

Flying instruction is also provided. In late 1939 Muncie Aviation started training pilots in conjunction with Ball State Teachers College. During World War II the training involved 1,600 Army and Navy officer cadets being instructed in 33 aircraft.

R.J. WHITINGER & COMPANY

Ralph J. Whitinger founded the certified public accountant firm, R.J. Whitinger & Company, in 1930.

The demand for public accountants was relatively small when Ralph Judson Whitinger graduated from Ball State Teachers College in 1929 and opted to enter that business field, opening his office in a building at 114 South Franklin Street on January 1, 1930.

The Muncie native ignored a lethargic economy just as he had previously overcome a physical handicap. Crippled by polio as a child, he offset a physical weakness with enormous strength of character.

Later he would observe that Muncie in 1930 was not a bad place and time to begin an accounting practice. The city had a larger than average concentration of home-owned industries. Legislation enacted in the near future would greatly increase the need for accounting services.

Still later, Whitinger's associates would note that it was often not circumstance, but his own business acumen, that enabled Whitinger to appear to be in just the right place at just the right time.

Federal income taxes were an established fact by 1930 but the withholding of taxes was yet to come. Social Security was effected in 1936. In 1933 a Federal Securities Act was passed requiring audits of publicly held companies. In that same year Indiana enacted a gross income tax and an intangibles tax.

Over a span of 50 years Whitinger's accounting business grew, from one room to virtually a quarter block, filling the structure at 114 South Franklin and the second floor of the facility next door on the southeast corner of Franklin and Main streets. Part of the first floor of that building, at 219 West Main, is occupied by Data Management Services, a Whitinger affiliate.

Whitinger received his CPA certificate in 1938. In 1949 he served as president of the Indiana Association of Certified Public Accountants, and he noted that only 18 of Indiana's 97 counties had CPAs at that time. To some extent the growth of R.J. Whitinger & Company has paralleled the general growth of CPA professionals in bringing ever-widening services to their clients.

R.J. Whitinger & Company became a partnership in 1945 when another CPA was brought in to be in charge of auditing. Records of the firm show that it then had a total of 11 employees, including the two principals. A third partner was added in 1947. The firm's business broadened from its early concentration on tax matters, offering auditing, estate planning, and management advisory services in addition.

These services remain the major categories of public accounting practiced by R.J. Whitinger & Company. The 1983 firm had 7 partners, 15 professional staff members, and 10 support staff personnel. These employees represent a considerable breadth and depth of experience in all areas of service provided by the firm.

Whitinger's own active participation in the firm decreased substantially in the years prior to his death in 1982, but the basic philosophies and standards he established for his practice were unchanged by the partners who succeeded him. He personally served as a director of several business firms; three foundations, among them Ball State University Foundation, of which he was president; and many civic and charitable organizations, including the United Way, of which he was a

founder and first president.

He received an honorary doctorate from Ball State and the school's College of Business building was named in his honor. A Whitinger Scholars' Program was established during his lifetime to honor 16 freshman students each year with a $1,500 annually renewable scholarship.

It is traditional that Whitinger partners have joined the firm to serve for a period of time before being admitted to full partnership. Some have joined and later completed their CPA examinations. Others have had considerable prior service with national CPA firms, corporations, or the Internal Revenue Service before joining R.J. Whitinger & Company. It is not required nor has it been the practice of the firm at any time to require a Ball State University degree as a prerequisite to partnership. Given Ralph Whitinger's loyal devotion to his alma mater, however, it is not surprising that the seven partners of this firm in 1983 are all BSU alumni!

The current partners continue the Whitinger tradition of involvement in the community. Collectively they are found on boards of financial institutions and local business corporations, charities, clubs, and civic associations. They also serve in professional organizations where their expertise is shared with peers in the state and in the nation.

R.J. Whitinger & Company conducts seminars for clients and the general public from time to time, to discuss changing regulations or the consequences of new legislation. In 1984 the firm counted 1,900 organizations, companies, and individuals among its current clients, making R.J. Whitinger & Company the largest CPA firm in the city.

MUNCIE FEDERAL SAVINGS AND LOAN ASSOCIATION

The Muncie Federal Savings and Loan Association, organized on April 1, 1889, is Delaware County's oldest financial institution. Today many individual loans and savings accounts far exceed the $15,000 in total assets reported at the end of this firm's first year in business.

Assets grew to more than $140 million by the end of 1983. During these 95 years, Muncie Federal has loaned hundreds of millions of dollars to purchase, build, or remodel homes in Delaware and surrounding counties.

Savings and loan associations, which were patterned after the building societies of England, became this country's main source of home financing in the early 1900s. While insured savings and home lending remain as main services offered by Muncie Federal in the 1980s, recent congressional deregulation of financial institutions has prompted a broadening of these services. This progressive institution now offers a variety of savings plans and loan programs to meet the changing needs of its customers.

Muncie Federal paid its first

Delaware County's oldest existing financial institution started here, at 119 West Jackson Street, on April 1, 1889.

dividend to savers in December 1889 and earnings have been paid without interruption ever since. Savings services include interest-bearing checking accounts paying day-in-to-day-out interest, high-yielding certificates of deposit, money market deposit accounts, and regular savings plans. Muncie Federal has joined the Inteller network of automatic teller machines providing customer access to statement savings and checking accounts day or night, at over 45 locations throughout Indiana.

Since its organization in the offices

of Chapman, Ream & Co. at 119 West Jackson Street, Muncie Federal has been located at four different downtown sites. A few years after the first meeting, the association constructed an apartment building and business complex on the southeast corner of Adams and High streets, maintaining its office there until 1925 when it moved to the former Delaware County National Bank Building on the northeast corner of Walnut and Main streets. Both of these buildings have since been razed. The present quarters, at the northeast corner of Charles and High streets, were occupied in January 1961.

In 1934 an act of Congress established the federal agencies which provide insurance of accounts in financial institutions. In order to offer that insurance to its savers, the association, which had been known as the Muncie Savings & Loan Company, became the third such association in the nation to obtain its federal charter.

The association opened its first branch office in Portland in 1974. Now there are also two branches and a free-standing Inteller installation in Muncie. More than 70 persons are currently employed in Muncie Federal's four offices.

City electric streetcar lines were being installed when this photo was taken looking southeast from the old county courthouse (circa 1895). The building at the extreme left became the home of Muncie Federal Savings and Loan from 1925 to 1961.

The current home of Muncie Federal Savings and Loan Association was first occupied in 1961 at Charles and High streets.

MUNCIE POWER PRODUCTS, INC.

Hamer D. Shafer has a right to be proud of Muncie Power Products, Inc., which he serves as board chairman. One of three employees when the company was first formed, Shafer has seen this firm grow to 90 employees in 1983. About half of these work in some 54,000 square feet of floor space between Pershing and Hackley streets south of Wysor, and the rest are divided among nine sales and distribution centers in Atlanta, Chicago, Dallas, Denver, Kansas City, Los Angeles, Orlando, Seattle, and Toledo.

Muncie Power Products started as an auto parts shop owned by Lou Conne on Eighth Street east of Hoyt in 1935. Known as Muncie Parts Mfg. Co. for much of its life, the firm has seen several transformations in the

These changes were the result of a team effort, and Shafer quickly shares his pride—and is moving to share the company—with the team members. Some 25 employees now own about 48 percent of the firm's stock in a deliberate move toward employee ownership.

"We looked for a force for change, and it was us," says president Joseph E. Wilson of the firm's move to develop its own product lines. Born in 1942, Wilson typifies the young leadership

Milestones in the company's history include a move to 2601 South Jefferson Street in 1945; Shafer's partnership with Frances Conne following the death of her father, Lou, in 1952; the move to the present site in 1959; and a new corporation organized by Shafer and Ralph Whitinger following

Hamer D. Shafer is seen in the Muncie Power Products warehouse and distribution center adjoining the company's headquarters at 342 North Pershing Drive.

This Powerflex power take-off (PTO) unit provides 27 to 54 horsepower at 1,000 r.p.m. with torques from 140 to 285 foot-pounds. This performance range previously required seven different PTO models in larger housings.

process of becoming a nationally recognized source of auxiliary power systems for truck-mounted material-handling equipment. In recent years it has moved from being basically a distributor of other companies' products to having a 99-percent proprietary product line of power equipment designed, engineered, and built to Muncie's own specifications.

team which continues to look ahead to still more changes in meeting the needs of truck equipment owners for state-of-the-art auxiliary power units.

Mechanical, pneumatic, and hydraulic equipment respond to control systems which now include sophisticated electronic circuitry. During 1982 Muncie Power Products moved to assure its continuing position as a leader in this field by acquiring an ownership position in one of its supplier firms, Diversified Systems, Inc., a high-tech electronics firm located in Indianapolis.

Frances Conne's death in 1966. Shafer considers 1966 a major turning point toward specialization in auxiliary truck equipment. The company's name change followed in 1979.

Power take-off units, pumps, and related equipment have carried Muncie's name into many industries, municipal, utilities, farming, mining, oil fields, construction, and over-the-road haulers throughout the nation. A new generation of employee ownership is expected to continue the pioneering traditions of Muncie Power Products.

INDUSTRIAL TRUST & SAVINGS BANK

The May-June 1982 issue of *Corporate Design* magazine showed part of Muncie's downtown Walnut Plaza reflected in the dark glass facade of the Industrial Trust & Savings Bank. This building has attracted national recognition and awards since its opening in 1980.

But Industrial Trust & Savings Bank is more than an impressive building. The institution prefers to be recognized most for the services it provides to people. Early advertising for this bank spoke of its dedication to "the man on the street." That attitude continues. When the PBS television series *Middletown* depicted a family business struggling for survival in the early '80s, Industrial Trust was recognized as the bank that provided rescue in the form of a Small Business Administration loan.

Among several "firsts" claimed by the bank is its introduction of charge account services in 1953—the first in Muncie and one of the first in Indiana. The system started with paper, then anodized aluminum, and then a plastic card as Industrial Trust joined the Midwest bank-card program and from that regional concept moved into the national MasterCard service. The charge account service started within four years of the firm's becoming a chartered bank.

Images of buildings on Mulberry Street reflect from the east facade of Industrial Trust & Savings Bank. © 1980 Paul Warchol, Esto Photographics Inc.

The bank's founder, Charles V. Sursa, had developed a successful insurance business in Muncie when, in 1927, he was encouraged by friends to open an industrial loan company. The Muncie Industrial Company was located at 117 East Adams Street, where it weathered the Depression years and grew until 1946, when Sursa applied for a state commercial bank charter. Gaining that charter in 1948, and opening in 1949 as the Industrial Trust & Savings Bank, consummated a major goal in the life of the founder, who died from a sudden heart attack in 1951.

David Sursa, son of the founder, had been trained in the banking field at

---

The heart of Industrial Trust's building, which opened in 1980, is a three-story atrium skylighting teller stations and a reception area surrounded by perimeter offices. © 1980 Paul Warchol, Esto Photographics Inc.

the Harvard University School of Business Administration. The bank's directors named him to succeed his father at age 26—one of the youngest bank presidents in the nation. (A third-generation Sursa, Charles V., son of David, was named vice-president in the commercial loan department in 1983.)

Under David Sursa's leadership, the bank has added three Muncie branches and merged with state banks in Yorktown and Albany to establish branches there. Bank assets have grown to nearly 100 times the approximately $1.5 million reported in 1949, and employment has risen from 18 in that year to 118 in 1983.

Industrial Trust & Savings Bank's headquarters literally reflects its surroundings. Its performance reflects its historic desire to be recognized first for the services it provides to people.

BALL STORES, INC.

Ball Stores was established in 1934 when the Ball Brothers, feeling that Muncie should have a quality department store, founded the store as an independent retail operation designed to cater to the needs of the people of eastern Indiana. The store, formerly occupied by the McNaughton Company, was located in a five-story building constructed in 1901 on the southeast corner of Charles and Walnut streets.

In 1938 Fred J. Petty, a vice-president and director of Ball Brothers Company, and his wife, Margaret Ball Petty, purchased the store from Ball Brothers Company. Ball Stores has operated as an independent department store in Indiana specializing in quality merchandise.

Mrs. Petty assumed the presidency of the firm after Fred Petty's death in 1949, continuing a program of improvement and remodeling begun by her husband. In 1951 Ralph C. Chase joined Ball Stores as merchandise manager and shortly afterwards was appointed chief executive officer.

Chase continued in the capacity of general manager and Ball Stores experienced a period of sustained growth and remodeling. In 1965 Edmund F. Petty became president and Ball Stores' growth continued with the purchase of a women's specialty store, the Collegienne Shops located near Ball State University, in 1968. A branch store opened at the Muncie Mall in 1978.

Martin Clark, formerly with Federated Department Stores, was appointed president of Ball Stores in 1982.

Ball Stores has long been a dominant factor in Muncie and the eastern Indiana community. The original objectives of quality and service have continued to be the basic cornerstones that express the ideals that best represent Ball Stores as it is and as it will be in the future.

—Edmund F. Petty

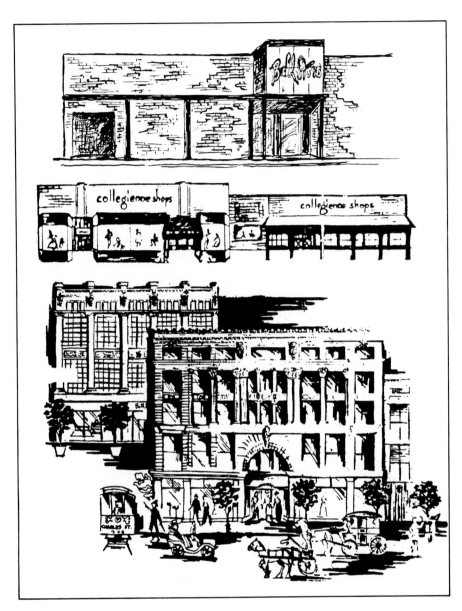

Shown here (from top to bottom) are the various stages of Ball Stores going back in time with the 1978 opening of a branch store at the Muncie Mall; a women's specialty store, the Collegienne Shops, purchased in 1968; and the original Ball Store, at Charles and Walnut streets, constructed in 1901 and occupied by the Ball Stores since 1934.

PERSHING'S GARDEN AND FLORIST

From 1879 to 1957 this shop at 205 North High Street was the predecessor of Pershing's Garden and Florist. Photo by Richard Greene.

World War I was over when the descendants of Frederick Pershing, or Pfoerching, met in 1923 to dedicate a monument in Westmoreland County, Pennsylvania, to this pioneer Alsatian emigrant. It is not surprising that General John J. Pershing was selected to make the dedicatory address.

Among those attending was Olynthus Howard Pershing of Muncie, proprietor of a seed business established in 1879. O.H. Pershing's father, David, was a Westmoreland County native who at one time had an interest in newspapers including the *Muncie Times,* and who later established a mercantile business selling seeds and provisions. David Pershing also lived in Rochester, Indiana, where he served as Fulton County auditor, and it was in Rochester that O.H. Pershing was born, in 1852.

The disposition of David Pershing's seed and grocery business in Muncie is not clear, and there is a possibility that his son's retail venture was an outgrowth of this early Muncie enterprise. Early histories also indicate that O.H. Pershing ran the Opera House Grocery at Main and Walnut streets before opening Pershing's Seed Store at 205 North High. What is certain is that the store in what has since become a law office would continue in that location for more than 70 years, passing from O.H. Pershing to his son, Ernest Howard Pershing, and eventually to a grandson, Robert Wynne Pershing, who with his wife Alyce relocated the store to 4205 North Wheeling Avenue in 1957.

The third-generation storeowners retired in 1969, and after a period of interim ownership the business was purchased by Paul and Wanda Zedekar in 1973. Paul is the son of the late James Zedekar, longtime principal of Emerson School, near which O.H. Pershing many years previously had owned a six-acre garden adjoining the Pershing residence on Ashland Avenue. James Zedekar's wife Huelda has a continuing interest in the enterprise now headed by her son and daughter-in-law.

The business includes a florist shop and a complete garden center, with bulk quality seeds as part of its stock. The Zedekars continue the business philosophy voiced by O.H. Pershing in a 1936 interview published by the *Seed Merchants* trade journal. The 83-year-old founder of Pershing's Garden and Florist then said: "I made up my mind a long time ago that when a man plants something, he expects it to grow; and instead of selling the kind of seed that price alone would sell, I reasoned that I would stock only No. 1 grade and I've stuck to that for nearly 50 years."

Pershing's Garden and Florist has been located at 4205 North Wheeling Avenue since 1957.

MUNCIE DISTRICT/INDIANA-AMERICAN WATER COMPANY, INC.

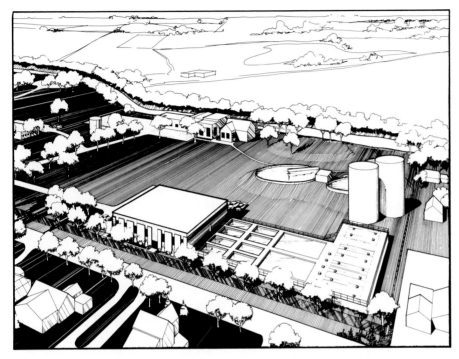

The Indiana-American Water Company, Inc., water treatment (center right and foreground), pumping, and distribution facilities (left). The treatment facility (foreground) was constructed in 1983 to replace facilities built over 80 years ago.

The Muncie District of the Indiana-American Water Company, Inc., in 1984, owned 302 miles of pipeline, 3,500 acres of land around the seven-billion-gallon Prairie Creek reservoir, two elevated tanks that hold three million gallons of water, and a production facility capable of treating over 20 million gallons of water per day.

Muncie District manager Ronald H. Moon estimates the replacement value of Muncie's water facilities at about $64 million. The original cost was about $25 million. Included is a $6.5-million water-treatment facility, completed in 1983 and built on the site of the city's original plant between Burlington Drive and the White River.

Indiana-American is a subsidiary of American Water Works Company, Inc., which was formed in 1947 with the Muncie utility as one of its original components. Local citizens organized the first water company to serve Muncie, but their interests were sold to a New York-based holding company in the early 1900s.

On January 19, 1885, the City of Muncie entered into a contract with Samuel A. Wilson, Abbott L. Johnson, Theodore F. Rose, and Samuel M. Highlands. These men were to organize a joint stock company to provide water for Muncie. The firm, capitalized at $100,000, began pumping in October 1885 from a well field on South Brotherton Street. In 1889 new wells were added along Burlington Drive and soon after that water was pumped and treated from the White River.

The city's growth, spurred by new industry attracted by the gas boom, may have been underestimated. Certainly one of the water company's major problems was not anticipated. When area gas wells started pumping salt instead, the brackish run-off into White River contaminated the city's water supply and river pumping was suspended from 1905 to 1916. During that time a new pumping station was built on Buck Creek.

By 1918 the city's original water contract was surrendered and the system was sold. Service has since been provided on an indeterminate permit. Gone forever are the contract rates fixing residential tap fees at six dollars a year, and use charges at 15 cents per 1,000 gallons. (The 1984 rate for 1,000 gallons was about $3.22.)

While the rates have changed drastically, so has the water system. And there are other benefits. Thanks to its water company, Muncie has one of the largest city parks in the Midwest, at Prairie Creek Reservoir in southeastern Delaware County. Ground adjoining the 1,250-acre reservoir, completed in 1962, was leased to the city for $10. The lease expires in 2021.

Muncie Water Works Company's (now Indiana-American Water Company, Inc.) filter building was constructed to process water from the White River to meet demands resulting from the growing population, which increased from 8,000 to over 20,000 due to the discovery of natural gas in the area. Photo circa 1900.

WOODLAND NURSING HOMES, INC.

The large one-story building at 3820 West Jackson Street is obviously a health care facility. But for a period of time each week its long front hall becomes a bowling alley—with regulation-size balls and pins, but, alas, no automatic pinsetter!

Residents of the 92-bed facility are participants, spectators, and owners of the bowling equipment. Many also belong to a "galloping gourmet" group, going out for special meals once a month. When National Nursing Home Week is observed, the occupants of this cheerful place gather for a balloon lift, placing a name and address in each balloon. Responses have come from balloon finders as far away as Cincinnati.

The official name of this facility is Woodland Nursing Homes, Inc., recalling a time when it was physically in two locations, both remodeled family dwellings, operating separately but with shared administration. It is not a chain.

In the beginning, 37 years ago, one woman, Hazel Wilson, R.N., was nurse, cook, and housekeeper here. She opened the first Woodland Nursing Home at 917 East Main Street in 1947, in partnership with Carroll Shroyer, also a nurse, who was employed until her retirement by an area industrial plant. The second home, at 1612 West Jackson, was

This was the original Woodland Nursing Home at 917-923 East Main Street from 1947 to 1968. Photo by Ruth Chin Photography.

added in 1961. Together they provided space for 42 patients.

The two homes were sold and patients moved in July 1968 to the present location, then a 68-bed facility. This was enlarged by 24 beds in 1972, and an activity room was also added later. A 30-bed addition was in the planning stage in late 1983.

Mrs. Wilson remains chairman of the board in Woodland Nursing Homes, where Anna Powless has been administrator since March 1, 1981. Mrs. Wilson's son, Gene, and Carroll Shroyer are co-owners. The firm employs 90 to 95 persons, including 17 licensed nurses (R.N.s and L.P.N.s). The director of nurses, Wilma Frazee, R.N., has been with the home since the present building opened in 1968. An assistant director, Marilyn Miller, R.N., was named when the new wing was added in 1972.

The home provides skilled and intermediate care and is eligible for Medicare and Medicaid. Independently owned by natives of Delaware County, Woodland encourages continuing community involvement. Several residents are members of the Retired Seniors Volunteer Program. And, during the American Heart Fund drive, Woodland residents hold an annual "Rock-and-Roll Jamboree"—taking pledges for rocking chair and rolling wheelchair distance and endurance races.

Today Woodland Nursing Homes is a 92-bed facility at 3820 West Jackson Street. A 30-bed addition is in the planning stage. Photo by Ruth Chin Photography.

DeFUR, VORAN, HANLEY, RADCLIFF & REED

The offices of DeFur, Voran, Hanley, Radcliff & Reed in the Indiana Gas Company building reflect a contemporary openness. Nothing would suggest the long history of the firm, which dates back to 1904.

The law firm of DeFur, Voran, Hanley, Radcliff & Reed is housed in contemporary fourth-floor offices in the Indiana Gas Company building at Jackson and Mulberry streets. There is nothing in the appearance of this firm to suggest that it dates to a 1904 office in the old Muncie Federal building on the northeast corner of Main and Walnut. There is nothing in the name of the firm to suggest that it originated with Adolph Silverberg and Leonadus "Lon" Bracken, who were joined in 1907 by Myron H. Gray.

The historic continuity may be more evident in the nature of the practice itself, the clients served, and the involvement of the firm's members in community affairs and charitable causes.

Adolph Silverberg, a native of Mississippi, established himself as a civic leader in Muncie until his death in 1928. Lon Bracken left the firm in 1915 to become secretary of the Federal Trade Commission in Washington, D.C. He subsequently held several other public posts.

Lon's place in the organization was taken by a brother, Tom, and eventually three generations of Brackens would be associated with this firm. Tom's son, Alexander M. Bracken, joined in 1931 but left after two years to join Ball Corporation, later serving that company as chairman of the board. Frank Bracken, son of Alex, entered the law firm in the 1960s but left to become solicitor general in the U.S. Department of the Interior. Frank returned to Muncie and joined Ball Corporation also.

Myron Gray was active in labor legislation and served on the committee that wrote the Indiana Financial Institutions Act. Marshall E. Hanley, whose name remains in the firm's title, was a partner from 1954 until his death in 1981. He served as a U.S. district attorney and was a candidate for the U.S. Senate.

Earl DeFur, who served as senior partner for many years, is now retired. Current active partners include Reed D. Voran, William F. Radcliff, Samuel L. Reed, Richard D. Hughes, Jon H. Moll, John C. Gilliland II, Gregory A. Huffman, and Steven D. Murphy. Current associate lawyers are Ted R. Brown and Thomas C. Pence. All are involved in civic activities and Sam Reed has been both a state representative and a U.S. magistrate.

The firm in 1983 had 12 attorneys, a legal administrator, two paralegals, and a dozen other staff members. In addition to a general civil practice, other areas of practice include labor and personnel relations, health care and hospital law, college and university law, pension and estate planning, taxation, banking, civil litigation, and real estate. Several of the county's major institutions and businesses are among the clients of DeFur, Voran, Hanley, Radcliff & Reed.

CHEVROLET-MUNCIE

In 1908 two events took place that became major milestones in automotive history. Henry Ford announced the Model T, and William C. Durant, then president of the Buick Motor Company, organized a firm called General Motors.

History has accorded Ford the wider personal recognition, although Buick built 8,478 cars in 1908 to Ford's 6,181. Durant's relatively obscure role may be due to the fact that his business career was far more volatile, contro-versial, and complex. He was a prolific originator and purchaser of companies.

In little more than a year Durant consolidated over 20 companies into General Motors, including Buick, Olds, Cadillac, and Oakland (later Pontiac). Then, in 1910, he lost control of the concern. He aided a Swiss auto racer and engineer, Louis Chevrolet, in yet another new venture, making light cars which became very popular. By 1916 Durant regained the helm in General Motors largely through trading Chevrolet Motor Company stock for that of GM.

Chevrolet was thus merged into General Motors, which Durant headed

Employees of the Chevrolet-Muncie Manual Transmission Plant inspect the new Pontiac Fiero sports car, which features Muncie's FX-125 four-speed transaxle gear box.

for only four more years. During that time plans were made to build a new plant in Muncie (1919) and to acquire the Sheridan Motor Company (1920). Sheridan cars were made in Muncie just a few blocks from the new plant site.

The new plant was the Muncie Products Division of General Motors, supplying transmissions for Oakland, Pontiac, Oldsmobile, and GMC Truck. Alfred P. Sloan, Jr., a later president of GM, credits this plant in his auto-biography with developing large-volume production of synchromesh transmissions which were adopted throughout GM's auto lines between 1928 and 1932.

Shifting economic fortunes were indicated by an addition to the forge plant in 1929, followed in three years by the permanent closing of the Muncie Products Division. The plant, however, was reopened in 1935 by Chevrolet, after a strike closed that division's Toledo transmission plant. The Muncie plant has continued to provide transmissions for Chevrolet except for a period during World War II when it was used mainly for forging and machining aircraft parts. Forging operations in Muncie were discontinued in 1982.

The plant has been enlarged several times. When GM celebrated its 75th anniversary in September 1983, the Muncie plant occupied 1.2 million square feet on 62.5 acres. The plant currently manufactures manual trans-missions for the Chevrolet, Pontiac, Oldsmobile, Buick, and World Truck and Bus divisions of the corporation. Employment is about 1,300—down from a peak of 3,200 attained in August 1981—and plant officials estimate some $24.9 million a year is generated by Chevrolet-Muncie in wages, benefits, and taxes paid locally.

The Chevrolet-Muncie Manual Transmission Plant, as shown in a recent photograph, now encompasses 62.5 acres with 1.2 million feet of the latest high-technology facilities.

DELCO BATTERY PLANT,
DELCO REMY DIVISION, GMC

A modern 400,000-square-foot plant on a 100-acre site at the southwest edge of Muncie has the capacity to produce up to 14,000 maintenance-free batteries per day. The facility was opened by General Motors' Delco Remy Division in 1977 to replace an older facility which at one time was considered the largest battery plant in the world, and which in slightly less than 50 years had produced 150 million auto and truck batteries.

The original Muncie plant had been used to build Interstate automobiles, and later Sheridan automobiles. William C. Durant, who resigned as GM's president in 1920, took over the facility in 1921 to make Durant motor cars, but that product was short-lived. The plant stood empty in 1928 when Charles E. Wilson, head of the Delco Remy Division in Anderson, Indiana, and later a successor to the General Motors presidency, acquired it to make Delco batteries. He had been unable to obtain sufficient standby electric power in Anderson at that time.

Wilson (who would later become Secretary of Defense under President Eisenhower), Alfred P. Sloan, board chairman of GM in 1928, and William Knudsen, who preceded Wilson as president of GM, were among company dignitaries welcomed by Muncie's Chamber of Commerce in 1928 when the decision to locate in the idle auto plant on West Willard Street was first announced.

The decision to build batteries here was of major importance to GM. Prior to 1928 batteries had been supplied to the auto manufacturers, at less than cost, by four independent producers. These companies made up the difference in profit from sales of replacement batteries in the automotive after-market. Efficiencies in design and production were required to make Delco batteries cost-competitive for even GM's own auto divisions. The plan succeeded.

By 1934 the Muncie plant was supplying all GM cars and trucks. A second plant in New Jersey was opened. The six-volt, 13-plate battery which was standard in the early '30s evolved over the next two decades to a 12-volt system, and a California plant was opened in 1954. Delco became truly the nation's number-one battery in terms of units in use. Although Delco has retained its position of brand leadership, the new Muncie battery plant additionally manufactures units sold under approximately 20 different private labels.

Delco Battery at one time employed 1,500 persons in Muncie, but less than half this number were employed by the firm in 1983. Increased production and recalls of laid-off workers were noted, however, as auto sales appeared to be recovering from a deep recession.

The original Muncie plant, on West Willard Street (below), was acquired by the Delco Remy Division to produce Delco batteries for General Motors. Today the firm is located in this new facility (bottom) at 4500 South Delaware Road. The new plant produces the well-known Delco battery as well as approximately 20 different private labels.

UNIVERSAL ELECTRIC COMPANY, INC.

Three young men working in an Indianapolis motor repair shop in the 1920s dreamed of having a business of their own. That this business would become the largest independent electrical distributor in Indiana, and one of the top 100 in the United States, was beyond any of their expectations.

Louis Ehrlich, Luke Bracken, and Cliff Buennagel came to Muncie in 1929 and shared a bachelor apartment above a small repair shop at the rear of 211 North High Street. Their enterprise, Universal Electric Company, almost failed to survive the Great Depression. The area's inter-urban transportation system had been an early important customer, but was about to become a financial casualty. Cliff Buennagel recalls that he spent several days in the waiting room of the company president in Indianapolis, finally collecting most of the $3,200 owed to his struggling firm. The money was needed for survival.

Later in the 1930s Buennagel became accustomed to making Friday morning rounds to personally collect accounts receivable in order to meet payroll. In August 1935 Universal's seven employees shared a weekly total of $154.57. Ehrlich opted out of the business that year to start his own venture.

Universal incorporated in 1936 and expanded into wholesaling electrical industrial supplies. Expansion, acquisitions, and relocation during the next 45 years gradually transformed the company. By 1980 Universal represented some 150 electrical manufacturers and its total sales neared $14 million. Employment peaked at 130 in the late 1970s. By 1984 there were 90 employees and the weekly payroll exceeded $25,000.

Facilities collectively worth more than $1.5 million were located in Muncie, Marion, Anderson, Richmond, New Castle, Kokomo, and Kendallville, Indiana, and in Lima, Ohio. More than 25 employees are also

stockholders, and the board of directors is entirely comprised of employees.

Bob Heavenridge, the first full-time employee hired by the original partners in 1934, succeeded Buennagel

Seen in this 1980 photograph are the officers of Universal Electric Company: (standing, left to right) Donald R. Buennagel, president, and Lowell Moore, vice-president. Seated (left to right) are Richard Perkins, secretary/treasurer, and Cliff Buennagel, founder and board chairman.

as company president from 1967 through 1976. Don Buennagel, Cliff's son, has been president since that time.

Universal was one of the first in its

field to use electronic data processing, starting in the early 1970s. It now has an in-house computer system.

The concern outgrew the entire building on North High Street when it expanded in 1936. It moved to 301

North High Street in 1939 and opened its first branch, in Marion, in 1940. Anderson was added in 1944 and Richmond in 1947. The Muncie operations relocated to 1601 South Walnut Street in 1952, later expanding south and west in the same block. In 1975 the corporate offices of Universal Electrical Company, Inc., were built at 1620 South High Street at 10th Street.

YOUNG MEN'S CHRISTIAN ASSOCIATION (YMCA)

Since its founding the YMCA has changed in response to prevailing needs, developing social, health-related, and recreation programs aimed at the enrichment of lives and concern for the total person.

Since 1975 the Muncie YMCA has occupied facilities on the southeast corner of Mulberry and Howard streets which serve thousands of area residents and are shown with pride to the city's visitors.

The YMCA building on the southwest corner of Adams and Jefferson streets similarly served as a busy center of community and recreational activities from 1914 to 1974. But this structure, now razed, was probably the third Muncie home for the YMCA, which was officially organized on July 20, 1880.

A history of the early "Y" was written by Dr. Hugh A. Cowing and placed in the cornerstone of the building at Adams and Jefferson. It lists the founding officers as A.W. Clancey, president; Joseph A. Goddard, vice-president; and J.M. Little, secretary.

On October 11, 1881, the association rented a large storeroom at the northwest corner of Walnut and Charles streets. This was "home" until 1893, when the First Baptist Church was enlarged and a YMCA gymnasium and reading rooms were

included in the basement of its new addition.

The building, opened in 1914, was two years in construction and cost more than $200,000. A fund drive was held in 1911 and the Ball brothers pledged to contribute $100,000 toward the needed amount. President William H. Taft visited Muncie on July 3, 1911, and exhorted the citizens to reach their goal. Before midnight the total amount

Occupying many homes since its beginning in 1880, the Young Men's Christian Association has now consolidated all its activities in this new facility at 500 South Mulberry Street.

raised was $109,000.

The YMCA opened a branch on South Madison Street in 1964, but this was sold to the City of Muncie in 1975 when all activities were consolidated in the new YMCA building.

The first Muncie YMCA resident camp was held at Idlewold Lake in June 1915. Next year the camp moved to Lake Wawasee. In 1917 the camp relocated to Little Tippecanoe Lake, where it purchased property four years later. Renamed Camp Crosley, its facilities have since served more than 60,000 youth and are currently being renovated and expanded through a five-year development program.

Since its founding in 1880 the YMCA has changed in response to current social needs, developing parent-child clubs called Indian Guides and Indian Princesses, before- and after-school child care centers, health-enhancement programs, corporate fitness and cardiovascular health programs, and providing sports such as basketball, volleyball, gymnastics, and swimming. What has not changed is the YMCA's historic commitment to Christian principles, and its goal of enriching the lives of people through concern for the total person.

131

GARDENS OF MEMORY

Gardens of Memory became a state-chartered nonprofit cemetery association on November 10, 1954. Its founder, Frank Randall, a 50-year-old native of Gaston, was coming back to Delaware County from Chicago and Dixon, Illinois.

Although governed by nine directors, all lot owners, the association, which now has 18 to 20 employees, still has some aspects of a family firm. Frank Randall has been joined in the business by three sons: Robert L. Randall, vice-president and general manager; Richard A. Randall,

The handcrafted, wrought-iron gazebo is the centerpiece of the Gardens of Love and Psalms and overlooks a large part of Gardens of Memory.

1981, to assure control of adjacent land areas and provide for future expansion. The site north of Royerton on State Road 3 was a wheat field when Randall first saw and purchased it, converting it into 17 separate garden areas each with its own central feature. All individual memorials are placed level with the lawn. Vaults are manufactured on the premises, and newer areas have been constructed with lawn crypts already in place, in advance of need.

The idea of a park-like cemetery with memorials level with the lawn was new to this area in 1954, but Randall had pioneered just such a concept at Dixon, Illinois, where he had founded and developed Chapel

The Tower of Miracles depicts three of Christ's miracles: calming the storm, feeding the multitude, and healing the blind. Carvings at the base of each pillar illustrate these events.

and build a park-like cemetery.

Randall taught school in Gaston and Matthews after graduating from Ball State, but he turned to accounting when he moved to Chicago in the 1920s. He worked for Montgomery Ward and Butler Paper Company, but "moonlighted" in accounting for three cemeteries, and thus became interested in cemetery management.

Friends from Muncie visiting in Dixon encouraged Randall's return to Delaware County. The success that followed this decision may be measured in terms of the growing assets of an endowment fund that assures perpetual care at Gardens of Memory. That irrevocable fund had grown to more than $1,750,000 by 1983.

Today carillon music emanates from two towers over Gardens of Memory. A 1,400-crypt chapel mausoleum was opened in 1966. More additions are being planned. And Frank Randall has found the satisfaction of his lifetime "by creating something everlasting where there was nothing before."

CPA, director and advisor to trustees; and Donald E. Randall, director and superintendent of grounds.

The original 63 acres have been supplemented by 21 acres purchased in 1972, and 88 acres purchased in

Hill Memorial Park several years earlier. Randall also became a licensed funeral director and built a funeral home at that cemetery, which was very successful; however, he had a tremendous desire to come back home

From the Swift collection.
Courtesy, Ball State University

Looking Toward 2000

Much of Delaware County's investment in its future—its youth— has been in education. Kindergarten classes were inaugurated in Muncie city schools in the 1920s, and the misses Bertha Covalt, left background, and Bertha Stetter, right, conducted this class at Emerson School in 1923-1924. The two women formerly ran a private kindergarten in the First Universalist Church. Emerson School was built in the Riverside neighborhood, formerly a separate municipal corporation, after Riverside's merger into Muncie in 1918. From the author's collection

It is difficult to approach the future—or even the present—with an historical perspective.

When John S. Ellis wrote his *Complete History of Delaware County, Indiana,* in 1898, neither Muncie nor Delaware County had yet celebrated its diamond anniversary as an organized entity. Yet the landscape familiar to Mr. Ellis and his contemporaries was markedly different from the land-scape of some 75 years before. Settlements had been established and expanded, and the nearly impenetrable forest was gone. Muncie could be considered a metropolis with its approximately 20,000 residents, and there were other communities throughout the county's nearly 400 square miles that enjoyed the same amenities as the county seat: electricity, central heating, piped-in natural gas, city sewers, indoor plumbing, paved thoroughfares, and frequent public transportation. Mr. Ellis and his contemporaries, regardless of place of residence in the county, likewise could have participated in cultural organizations, clubs and lodges, and churches—in permanent buildings with educated men in the pulpit. Free public schools ran at least through the eighth grade and, if the pupils were able to get there, through high school. The Ellis history, however, was mainly of the land and those who occupied it. It did not deal with trends, political or economic issues, disasters, or successes, except perhaps in occasional passing mention.

Less than a decade later, Dr. G.W.H. Kemper, a respected Civil War veteran and longtime Muncie physician and surgeon, was the author of a two-volume *History of Delaware County* with a different approach. Dr. Kemper did not so much transcribe land entries as chronicle events. He depended on written and oral accounts of the past 80 years of Muncie and Delaware County, and he delved even into pre-settlement history through geological surveys and works of larger geographical scope.

Neither Ellis nor Kemper dealt with his contemporary situation with any degree of assurance. Ellis dealt with them a bit as he looked at present occupants of the land about which he wrote, and Kemper occasionally would become a civic booster of sorts in remarking on how different— and how much "better"—things were in the county of the early 1900s than they ever had been before. Neither man, however, looked at the many important trends that dominated the lives of Muncie and Delaware County residents then, let alone what might happen in the future. Ellis does not mention the gas boom or the development of public trans-portation or of civic public works over the preceding 25 years. Kemper mentions these, but he does not mention the automobile—which was already in what was then mass production in several American cities including Albany and Muncie—in the historical volume of his *History of Delaware County*.

Frank D. Haimbaugh's *History of Delaware County*, a two-volume work published in 1924, does not contain in its historical volume the abundance of chronological material available in Kemper's. Haimbaugh deals with growth patterns of Muncie and Delaware County and the progression of industrial development over the preceding 50 years. Again, no trends are viewed and no events are assigned significance ahead of others. It should be noted that Haimbaugh died as his work was being completed, but the tenor of his early chapters would indicate that no such broad appraisal of Muncie's present and future was planned beyond that which finally was printed. For example, by the mid-1920s the nation was carrying on a love affair with the automobile and the convenience it brought to everyday living. Yet the automobile is mentioned only in one brief passage near the end of the historical volume of Haimbaugh's work: he refers to a comment that he had made in 1896 as editor of the *Muncie Daily Herald*, predicting that automobiles, not yet seen in Muncie, would become commonplace within a decade. Would airplanes, wonders Haimbaugh in 1924, achieve the same commonality?

Having stated all of this by way of introduction, I would like to take a look at the present and toward the year 2000 for Muncie and Delaware County.

According to statistics and projections furnished by the Bureau of the Census, the days of pronounced population growth for Indiana and most other states of the central Midwest are over. Shifts in population are likely to continue through the balance of the 20th century, however, and if Delaware County is able to maintain its balance as an area engaged in manufacturing, agriculture, education, and human services, its importance to the state and nation will continue.

Also, residents of Muncie and Delaware County appear more tolerant in the 1980s. Although members of racial minorities continue to populate city and county at about the same percentages as in earlier decades of the century, there has been considerable change in how the majority perceives them and their problems. And although geographic segregation still exists, its effects have been watered down by school redistricting and political enlightenment. However, in the 1980s Muncie's black population still lacks a large professional community, which can be blamed primarily on the lack of opportunities for blacks in the area as compared with such opportunities in larger metropolitan centers.

In a 1983 address to members of the Muncie Rotary Club, Indiana's Lieutenant Governor John Mutz, also the state's commissioner of agriculture and head of the state's department of commerce, reflected on changing employment patterns. Mutz noted that neither the state nor the

Right: There was no retaining wall along White River when this picture of Wheeling Avenue was taken, probably in the late 1890s. Note the horse-drawn carriage and the streetcar. From the author's collection

Below right: Muncie had progressed rapidly in the 30 years that came after the above photograph was taken. Although the city was suffering from the Great Depression, Muncie's University Avenue near the new Ball Memorial Hospital (left) was lined with cars in the spring of 1932. From the Swift collection. Courtesy, Ball State University

Below far right: Financed partially by public subscription, in the mid-1960s a six-story addition was constructed on the east side of Ball Memorial Hospital's main building, providing additional bed space and better facilities for several hospital departments. Construction has long been a mainstay of Muncie's economy, and it appears that service industries like medical care will keep the economy strong into the 21st century. Courtesy, Ball Memorial Hospital

nation would likely ever see again the days when automobile manufacturing would dominate the economy as it had in the previous 60 years. Competitive pressures from abroad, changing technology, and changing markets were all to blame for that, he said. Mutz noted further that more and more Americans would be involved in service industries as opposed to the hands-on manufacturing of either hard or soft goods for consumer consumption. Thus, the lieutenant governor predicted that education would need to be directed toward retraining people who have been working in out-of-date industries, and that this retraining might be necessary as often as every decade or so.

Thus, Ball State University's development as a major educational institution in the half-century beginning in 1918 has placed Muncie in an advantageous position with regard to educational dominance in the final decades of the 20th century. The Indiana Legislature and the Ball State University Board of Trustees recognized in the 1970s that instruction in new disciplines for an age of information and service would be needed. A commitment to expanding the curriculum in such fields as computer science and electronic communications has extended into the 1980s, and such changes will likely continue as the needs of its potential students change in the years prior to 2000. Delaware County has also enjoyed since the 1960s a regional campus of Indiana Vocational Technical College (IVTC or Ivy Tech), which itself is responding in the 1980s to the needs of its communities for persons trained not only in technical fields but in health and human services as well.

During the 1970s and 1980s Ball Memorial Hospital, stabilized in size, also embarked on programs to improve itself as a regional medical center, supplementing services offered by independent medical specialists and mental health agencies. This trend is likely to continue well into the next century.

Muncie and Delaware County, then, can look toward the year 2000 expecting the following:

- Continued growth as an educational and medical center
- Renewed emphasis on teacher training at Ball State University and on technical education at both Ball State and Ivy Tech
- Continued specialization in agriculture (with farms growing larger, more modern, and more centrally managed, and in the same process less labor-intensive)
- Continued identification as a major manufacturing community, although with reduced manufacturing employment because of technological advances
- Further identification with other major population centers of the state as electronic communications tend to diminish geographic distances (for example, the Muncie-Anderson-Indianapolis area may find itself developing more as one unit and less as three distinct cities)
- Additional residential development in formerly productive agricultural

land in Delaware County, and

• Additional emphasis on quality secondary education in all of the school systems of the city and county, probably within the present physical facilities but with modifications to expand instruction in such new technologies as computer science and robotics.

Sociological studies done in Muncie in the 1970s have shown that the family unit is still intact and religious values are mostly unchanged from the time five decades earlier that the community was first studied by the Lynds. That being accepted, it would seem unlikely that—unless something like a major world crisis or a natural disaster occurred to change the community's course—serious changes in lifestyles or institutions could develop between the 1980s and 2000. It would appear that Delaware County has embarked upon its course for the future and will continue to grow, although in different directions, into the 21st century.

Patrons

The following individuals, companies, and organizations have made a valuable commitment to the quality of this publication. Windsor Publications and the Muncie-Delaware County Chamber of Commerce gratefully acknowledge their participation in *Muncie and Delaware County: An Illustrated Retrospective.*

Aircraft Distributors of Muncie, Inc.
Al Pete Meats, Inc.
Ball Corporation*
Ball Memorial Hospital*
Ball State University*
Ball Stores, Inc.*
Donald L. and Hope Barnes
Lawrence D. Benken, M.D.
A.E. Boyce Co., Inc.*
Broderick Co., Division of Harsco Corporation*
Mr. and Mrs. Gerald Chauvin
Chevrolet-Muncie*
DeFur, Voran, Hanley, Radcliff & Reed*
Delaware County Abstract Company*
Delco Battery Plant, Delco Remy Division, GMC*
DynAmerica, Inc.
Elm Ridge Cemetery*
J.C. Faris Sales, Inc.
John W. and Janice Ball Fisher
R.L. Floyd
Dr. Ted L. Fullhart
Gardens of Memory*
General GMC Truck Sales
Indiana & Michigan Electric Company
Indiana Vocational Technical College—Region Six*
Industrial Trust & Savings Bank*
Jack's Camera Shop, Inc.
Mr. and Mrs. Robert C. Keesling
Marsh Supermarkets, Inc.*
Maxon Corporation*
The Meeks Mortuary*
Merchants National Bank of Muncie*
Mid-West Towel and Linen Service, Inc.
Muncie Aviation Corporation*
Muncie District/Indiana-American Water Company, Inc.*
Muncie Federal Savings and Loan Association*
Muncie Power Products, Inc.*
Muncie Star and *Muncie Evening Press*
Mutual Federal Savings Bank
Mutual Home Federal Savings and Loan Association*
Ontario Corporation*
Pershing's Garden and Florist*
Universal Electric Company, Inc.*
Warner Gear*
Westinghouse Electric Corporation*
R.J. Whitinger & Company*
Woodland Nursing Homes, Inc.*
Young Men's Christian Association (YMCA)*
Ben Zeigler Company, Inc.*

*Partners in Progress of *Muncie and Delaware County: An Illustrated Retrospective.* The histories of these companies and organizations appear in Chapter Seven beginning on page 87.

This 1925 Muncie (Central) High School football team had an extremely successful season. Posing with the team at left is Coach Raymond Myrick. In the second row seated at right is Frank Allen, who later became Muncie schools superintendent, superintendent at South Bend, and finally athletic director of Indiana University. From the Swift collection. Courtesy, Ball State University

Bibliography

Abel, Mary Frances. *Revolutionary War Soldiers Buried in Delaware County.* Muncie: Daughters of the American Revolution, Paul Revere Chapter, 1976.

Atherton, Lewis. *Main Street on the Middle Border.* Bloomington: Indiana University Press, 1954.

Birmingham, Frederic A. *Ball Corporation—The First Century.* Indianapolis: Curtis Publishing Co., 1980.

Caplow, Theodore; Bahr, Howard; and Chadwick, Bruce. *All Faithful People: Change and Continuity in Middletown's Religion.* Minneapolis: University of Minnesota Press, 1983.

Caplow, Theodore, et al. *Middletown Families—Fifty Years of Change and Continuity.* Minneapolis: University of Minnesota Press, 1982.

Carmony, Donald F. *Handbook on Indiana History.* Indianapolis: Indiana Sesquicentennial Commission, 1963.

Carmony, Marvin; and Baker, Ronald L. *Indiana Place Names.* Bloomington: Indiana University Press, 1975.

Condran, John G., et al. *Working in Middletown: Getting a Living in Muncie, Indiana.* Muncie: Indiana Committee for the Humanities, J. Paul Mitchell, project director, 1976.

Dunn, John Piatt. *Indiana and Indianans.* Five volumes. Chicago and New York: American Historical Society, 1919.

Ellis, John S. *Complete History of Delaware County, Indiana.* Muncie: Neely Printing Co., 1898.

Emerson, Charles. *Muncie Directory for 1876-1877.* Muncie: The Muncie Weekly Times Steam Print, 1876.

Esarey, Logan. *A History of Indiana from its Exploration to 1850.* 1914. Reprint. Indianapolis: Hoosier Heritage Press, 1970.

Esarey, Logan. *A History of Indiana From 1850 to the Present.* 1914. Reprint. Indianapolis: Hoosier Heritage Press, 1970.

Furnas, J.C. *The Americans: A Social History of the United States, 1587-1914.* New York: G.P. Putnam's Sons, 1969.

Gray, Ralph D. *Alloys and Automobiles: The Life of Elwood Haynes.* Indianapolis: Indiana Historical Society, 1979.

Goodall, Hurley; and Mitchell, J. Paul. *A History of Negroes in Muncie.* Muncie: Ball State University, 1976.

Greene, Richard A. *Muncie and Delaware County: An Historical Sketch.* Muncie: Delaware County Historical Society, 1965.

Greene, Richard A. *The Story of Iron and Steel in Muncie.* Muncie: Muncie Chamber of Commerce, 1951.

Haimbaugh, Frank D., ed. *History of Delaware County, Indiana.* Two volumes. Indianapolis: Historical Publishing Co., 1924.

Hampton, Taylor. *The Nickel Plate Road.* Cleveland and New York: The World Publishing Co., 1947.

Helm, Thomas B. *History of Delaware County.* Chicago: Kingman Brothers, 1881.

Hermansen, David. *Indiana Courthouses of the Nineteenth Century.* Muncie: Ball State University, 1968.

Kemper, G.W.H., M.D., ed. *A Twentieth Century History of Delaware County, Indiana.* Two volumes. Chicago: Lewis Publishing Co., 1908.

Lingeman, Richard. *Small Town America.* New York: Houghton-Mifflin Co., 1981.

Lynd, Robert S., and Lynd, Helen Merrell. *Middletown.* New York: Harcourt, Brace and World, 1929.

Lynd, Robert S., and Lynd, Helen Merrell. *Middletown in Transition.* New York: Harcourt, Brace, Jovanovich, 1937.

Marlette, Jerry. *Electric Railroads of Indiana.* Indianapolis: Jerry Marlette, 1959.

McPhetridge, Lannes. *Delaware County in the World War, 1917-1918.* Indianapolis: Enquirer Printing and Publishing Co., 1919.

Peat, Wilbur D. *Portraits and Painters of the Governors of Indiana, 1800-1978.* Indianapolis: Indiana Historical Society, 1978.

Richter, Conrad. *The Awakening Land.* New York: Alfred A. Knopf, 1966.

White, Glenn. *The Ball State Story: From Normal Institute to University.* Muncie: Ball State University, 1967.

Whiteley, Amos. *The Whiteleys in America.* Muncie: Amos Whiteley, 1922.

_____. *A Portrait and Biographical Record of Delaware County, Indiana.* Chicago: A.W. Bowen and Co., 1894.

_____. *Indiana, A Guide to the Hoosier State.* WPA Writers Project, American Guide Series. New York: Oxford University Press, 1945.

Index

THIS BOOK WAS SET IN
PONTIAC TYPE,
PRINTED ON
MEAD OFFSET ENAMEL
AND BOUND BY
WALSWORTH PUBLISHING COMPANY.